S. HRG. 105–480

COMPREHENSIVE TEST BAN TREATY

HEARING

BEFORE A

SUBCOMMITTEE OF THE

COMMITTEE ON APPROPRIATIONS

UNITED STATES SENATE

ONE HUNDRED FIFTH CONGRESS

FIRST SESSION

SPECIAL HEARING

Department of Defense
Department of Energy

Printed for the use of the Committee on Appropriations

Available via the World Wide Web: http://www.access.gpo.gov/congress/senate

U.S. GOVERNMENT PRINTING OFFICE

48–165 cc WASHINGTON : 1998

For sale by the U.S. Government Printing Office
Superintendent of Documents, Congressional Sales Office, Washington, DC 20402
ISBN 0-16-057011-5

COMMITTEE ON APPROPRIATIONS

TED STEVENS, Alaska, *Chairman*

THAD COCHRAN, Mississippi
ARLEN SPECTER, Pennsylvania
PETE V. DOMENICI, New Mexico
CHRISTOPHER S. BOND, Missouri
SLADE GORTON, Washington
MITCH McCONNELL, Kentucky
CONRAD BURNS, Montana
RICHARD C. SHELBY, Alabama
JUDD GREGG, New Hampshire
ROBERT F. BENNETT, Utah
BEN NIGHTHORSE CAMPBELL, Colorado
LARRY CRAIG, Idaho
LAUCH FAIRCLOTH, North Carolina
KAY BAILEY HUTCHISON, Texas

ROBERT C. BYRD, West Virginia
DANIEL K. INOUYE, Hawaii
ERNEST F. HOLLINGS, South Carolina
PATRICK J. LEAHY, Vermont
DALE BUMPERS, Arkansas
FRANK R. LAUTENBERG, New Jersey
TOM HARKIN, Iowa
BARBARA A. MIKULSKI, Maryland
HARRY REID, Nevada
HERB KOHL, Wisconsin
PATTY MURRAY, Washington
BYRON DORGAN, North Dakota
BARBARA BOXER, California

STEVEN J. CORTESE, *Staff Director*
LISA SUTHERLAND, *Deputy Staff Director*
JAMES H. ENGLISH, *Minority Staff Director*

SUBCOMMITTEE ON ENERGY AND WATER DEVELOPMENT

PETE V. DOMENICI, New Mexico *Chairman*

THAD COCHRAN, Mississippi
SLADE GORTON, Washington
MITCH McCONNELL, Kentucky
ROBERT F. BENNETT, Utah
CONRAD BURNS, Montana
LARRY CRAIG, Idaho
TED STEVENS, Alaska *(ex officio)*

HARRY REID, Nevada
ROBERT C. BYRD, West Virginia
ERNEST F. HOLLINGS, South Carolina
PATTY MURRAY, Washington
HERB KOHL, Wisconsin
BYRON DORGAN, North Dakota

Staff

ALEX W. FLINT
W. DAVID GWALTNEY
LASHAWNDA LEFTWICH

CONTENTS

DEPARTMENT OF ENERGY

DEPARTMENT OF DEFENSE

DEPARTMENT OF ENERGY

COMPREHENSIVE TEST BAN TREATY

WEDNESDAY, OCTOBER 29, 1997

U.S. SENATE,
SUBCOMMITTEE ON ENERGY AND WATER DEVELOPMENT,
COMMITTEE ON APPROPRIATIONS,
Washington, DC.

The subcommittee met at 2:41 p.m., in room SD–124, Dirksen Senate Office Building, Hon. Pete V. Domenici (chairman) presiding.

Present: Senators Domenici, Cochran, Reid, and Dorgan.

DEPARTMENT OF ENERGY

STATEMENT OF HON. FEDERICO PEÑA, SECRETARY OF ENERGY

OPENING STATEMENT OF PETE V. DOMENICI

Senator DOMENICI. Could we have order, please?

We are going to try in the next 2 hours or slightly less to have two panels of witnesses on our subject matter, the Comprehensive Test Ban Treaty. The first will be Hon. Federico Peña, Secretary of Energy.

Then the panel following you, Mr. Secretary, will be Dr. Victor Reis, Assistant Secretary of Energy for Defense Programs; and Frank Miller, Acting Assistant Secretary of Defense for International Security Policy, to be accompanied by Dr. Harold Smith, Jr., Assistant to the Secretary of Defense for Atomic Energy.

I thank you all for coming and whoever is here in the audience, we appreciate your presence.

I thank the two Senators who are here on the Democratic side. My ranking member has exhibited as strong an interest in all of this as I have and I am most pleased that he can be here at this hearing. Frankly, as many Senators as can get a head start on this issue, the better off the proposal is and the better off we are as an Appropriations Committee.

This is the first hearing scheduled by the Energy and Water Development Subcommittee of Appropriations to explore how the Comprehensive Test Ban Treaty, if ratified, will impact the appropriation process for the Nation's defense and energy budgets.

I am expecting that we will determine major impacts both on DOE's Stockpile Stewardship and Management Program and on their verification programs on appropriations.

The President on September 22, transmitted the Comprehensive Test Ban Treaty to the Senate for our study and evaluation prior to consideration of providing consent to ratification of the treaty. While all treaty actions require careful evaluation, this particular treaty presents a most unique set of potential benefits and risks which will require unusual care in our deliberations and studies.

In the short time we have spent thus far in learning about it and attending other hearings on it, that last statement may even be an understatement.

The CTBT is directly relevant to the power of our nuclear stockpile as the ultimate deterrent force for preserving our country's freedom and global stability.

On a personal note, nuclear stockpile issues are the subject of intense interest and focus for me. I have worked at them, around them, and with this stockpile issue for almost 25 years, now.

In our hearing today, we are going to hear from the Secretary of Energy, Federico Peña, as our first panel, and I have already told you who will follow on the second one.

Now, I yield to the ranking member and to Senator Dorgan for any remarks they may wish to make.

STATEMENT OF HARRY REID

Senator REID. Mr. Chairman, this hearing is extremely important and I am glad that you have moved forward quickly to establish the guidelines and direction for this, I think one of the most important watershed events to come from the end of the cold war, that is, how do we make sure that our nuclear arsenal is safe and reliable.

Every president since President Eisenhower has maintained a nuclear arsenal to deter aggression, initially of the Soviet Union and later China, and it has worked.

Mr. Chairman, I have a statement that I would ask be made part of the record in its entirety. I am very anxious to get to the witnesses and my statement I think covers what needs to be covered.

PREPARED STATEMENT

I would ask your permission to have this made part of the record.

Senator DOMENICI. It will be made part of the record.

[The statement follows:]

PREPARED STATEMENT OF SENATOR HARRY REID

INTRODUCTION

The serious consideration being given all around the world to implementation of a treaty banning any and all nuclear explosions is a watershed event accompanying the end of the Cold War. For more than 50 years, the major nuclear powers founded their relationships on the very real possibility of a nuclear confrontation that might become uncontrollable. To prevent this catastrophe, each side established nuclear arsenals adequate to deter the other side from nuclear aggression. The moves and counter moves essential to maintaining this balance of deterrence required continuous modernization and replacement of stockpiled weapons on both sides. The testing of these new weapons for their respective stockpiles was, and is today, the only tried and true means of guaranteeing that the newly configured stockpile would be safe and effective, and would be perceived by the other side as effective, in maintaining the nuclear balance between the opposing superpowers.

Compliance with the Comprehensive Test Ban Treaty (CTBT) will deny confidence, formerly attained through testing, for the production and stockpiling of new nuclear weapon designs. This loss of confidence is believed adequate to inhibit new weapons development by both sides, effectively ending continuous stockpile improvements through modernization and replacement. Although a prohibition of any and all nuclear explosions cannot guarantee a prohibition of new weapons development (it only prohibits the testing of newly developed weapons), it will inhibit such development, and thereby will promote stabilization of existing nuclear arsenals.

Implementation of a Comprehensive Test Ban Treaty could promote confidence between former adversaries that cooperation without confrontation is possible. Such confidence could lead to further reductions in nuclear arsenals. The international example of refraining from nuclear testing, along with reductions in strategic stockpiles, could reduce incentives for nonnuclear states to develop their own nuclear explosives capabilities.

The likely cessation of unconstrained growth of nuclear weapons stockpiles and reduction of proliferation incentives among nonnuclear nations are benefits that are enabled by a Comprehensive Test Ban Treaty. A cost of these benefits is an unmeasurable reduction of confidence in the safety and reliability of our enduring stockpile. This cost arises because our past practices of testing for reliability, and of replacement of aging, unsafe weapons with new, tested designs will no longer be possible. It is essential that adequate confidence in stockpile safety and reliability be maintained through means other than testing because these weapons will continue to be the foundation of our strategic national security.

Advice and consent of the United States Senate regarding the Comprehensive Test Ban Treaty will generate a broad debate of its benefits and costs. As a part of that debate, it is important to recognize what the treaty provides, and what it does not provide.

The CTBT prohibits any and all nuclear explosions for any purpose, and thereby reduces confidence in stockpile safety and reliability unless some other means is found to maintain that confidence.

The CTBT does not prevent new nuclear weapons development; it only inhibits that activity. One of our earliest designs was used without testing, so that it is evident that weapons development can proceed without testing. However, the President of the United States has stated that the National Weapons Laboratories are prohibited from undertaking new weapons design activities. Moreover, United States weapons are highly sophisticated systems that perform at the very boundary of feasibility. It would be foolhardy in the extreme for the United States to attempt to incorporate a new design in its delivery systems without confirmatory testing. However, it needs to be recognized that other nations might risk the development of a weapon without testing. In this same spirit, the CTBT does not guarantee against modernization of existing stockpiles; it only makes such practice highly unlikely because new designs can not be tested for performance and safety. Again, the United States stockpile consists of highly sophisticated designs tailored to fit the existing delivery systems. Modernization of that stockpile without nuclear testing is not feasible.

The CTBT provides no guarantee of a total cessation of nuclear testing because compliance verification is very uncertain for all very low yield tests (less than about 100 tons) and for higher yield "decoupled" explosions. At the same time, it is possible for a signatory nation to execute a very high yield "unattended" explosion in a clandestine operation that could not be attributed to its originator. Whereas United States policy demands that it adhere to the letter and the spirit of international agreements that it is a party to, other signatory nations might not conduct their affairs with the same level of fidelity. It is important to recognize that it is technically possible to conduct a nuclear explosion that might not be detected or attributed with confidence.

The CTBT does not prevent nuclear proliferation; it only inhibits proliferation by possibly reducing proliferation incentives and by inhibiting or preventing development testing.

The Senate debate of the CTBT risks and benefits will address each of these issues. The following brief remarks will highlight what I believe to be the core elements of a few of these issues.

MAINTAINING SAFETY AND RELIABILITY OF THE U.S. NUCLEAR STOCKPILE

The nuclear weapons stockpile has been the foundation of U.S. national security for more than 50 years. It will likely remain so for the indefinite future. Although the Cold War has ended, there are still enormous stores of nuclear weapons in Russia, a country whose political and economic future remains uncertain. At the same time, China is a significant nuclear power with national interests that will not always be compatible with our own. For these and other reasons, the President has said, "* * * I consider the maintenance of a safe and reliable nuclear stockpile to be a supreme national interest of the United States."

The advent of a ban on nuclear testing was accompanied by the development of a plan to retain confidence in our nuclear stockpile for the indefinite future without nuclear testing. This plan relies on significant advances in scientific understanding and computer simulation of weapons performance to predict with confidence the state and character of our stockpile without testing. Its success depends critically on dramatic increases in computational performance and on dramatic increases in the resolution with which nonnuclear experiments can be measured.

The core issues of this so-called Stockpile Stewardship Program are the investments in computers and codes for advances in numerical simulation, and the investments in new experimental facilities to develop the data upon which the simulations will rely.

This year, the fiscal year 1998 appropriation for the Stockpile Stewardship Program was about 4.2 billion dollars, exceeding the Administration's request by about 200 million dollars. Subsequently, the Department of Energy, working with the Department of Defense and the National Weapons Laboratories, concluded that the stewardship program will require about 4.5 billion dollars per year for ten years, or 500 million dollars more per year than requested for fiscal year 1998.

The explanation for the differences between the original Administration request, the appropriation, and the subsequent determination of required funding is that the developers and executors of the stewardship plan are still learning about program requirements and their costs. This is a reasonable and believable explanation. Nevertheless, there is no guarantee that we have learned all we need to know to predict with confidence the exact content, schedule, and cost of the Stockpile Stewardship Program. In fact, it is more likely than not that we still have much to learn.

One of the "safeguards upon which the CTBT is conditioned mandates the stockpile stewardship program to ensure confidence in the safety and reliability of our nuclear stockpile." It is important that the Administration and the Congress recognize that the stewardship program is breaking new ground, "going where none have gone before", and we must be prepared and committed to providing the necessary resources for its success.

The Senate deliberations on the CTBT will doubtless explore the level of uncertainty in the stockpile stewardship plan, and will attempt to determine the levels of commitment to program success on the part of both the Congress and the Administration.

TEST READINESS

Another of the CTBT safeguards mandates the maintenance of the basic capability to resume nuclear testing should the United States withdraw from the treaty. Such withdrawal might be necessary if a nation ignores or violates the treaty, and, in so doing, disrupts the strategic balance in ways that might only be corrected through additions or replacements to our own stockpile.

Another safeguard acknowledges that the President, in consultation with Congress, is prepared to withdraw from the treaty in deference to our supreme national interest in maintaining a safe and reliable stockpile. This option could be activated if the Stockpile Stewardship Program concluded that it was unable to certify high confidence in the safety or reliability of a nuclear weapon type that is determined to be critical to maintaining our nuclear deterrent. This safeguard is rendered impotent if we do not faithfully ensure our readiness to resume testing if and when necessary.

I believe that a critical issue arises in test readiness. Should the United States identify a safety or reliability problem with a stockpile weapon type that prevents high confidence in the stockpile deterrent value, it could withdraw from the treaty under the "supreme national interests" clause. Withdrawal under these terms would permit the recovery of stockpile confidence by nuclear testing. Upon withdrawal, it might be concluded by another nation that the United States stockpile is ineffective. Therefore, during the period of time between treaty withdrawal and stockpile remedy through testing, an opponent might conclude that the United States is vulnerable to nuclear extortion or to nuclear attack. It is unacceptable to extend that window of real or perceived vulnerability by inadequately defining or funding a test readiness program.

During the Senate consideration of the CTBT, I am going to stimulate the development of a plan for test readiness that will ensure the absolute minimum delay between a decision to resume testing, and the actual resumption of testing.

COMPLIANCE VERIFICATION

It is self evident that verification of compliance with the CTBT is of paramount interest to all the signatory nations. Accordingly, a very comprehensive treaty verification effort has been mounted as a part of the treaty development. The International Monitoring System (IMS) addresses all the known local and remote signatures that would indicate that a nuclear explosion has occurred. A prototype data repository, called the International Data Center (IDC) has been developed to accumulate and integrate the data from the worldwide measurement sites of the IMS.

Whereas the IMS and IDC will provide formidable capability to detect a nuclear explosion, the system is not infallible. Very low yield explosions can be conducted anywhere without assured detection, and some geographic locations are better than others for clandestine testing in violation of the treaty. At the same time, there are evasive measures that permit much higher yield explosions without assured detection by elements of the IMS. Finally, it is possible for a nation to conduct a clandestine operation leading to an unattended nuclear detonation that could not be attributed to the source nation. In this case, all would know that a treaty violation occurred, but none would know which nation was responsible.

Whereas it is reasonable to assume that the strategic balance might not suffer from a single undetected test by one of the nuclear superpowers, such a test by an emerging nuclear capable state could provide that nation with confidence adequate to upset a local or regional balance of power.

The inability to verify with confidence that signatory nations are complying with the terms of the treaty is a serious deficiency. Such compliance uncertainty might be considered a fatal flaw. This deficiency would certainly make the treaty unacceptable if undetectable violations could lead to a disruption of nuclear deterrence. Both of these concerns must be explored during the coming debates.

CONCLUDING REMARKS

A Comprehensive Test Ban treaty would indeed be a watershed event deriving from the termination of the Cold War. Nevertheless, the CTBT does not provide all the things its proponents claim for it. It does assuredly prohibit all nuclear explosions for any purpose, but it does not appear to be conclusively verifiable under all conditions and for all prohibited activities.

A CTBT will necessarily reduce our confidence in the safety and reliability of our nuclear deterrent, but the developing Stockpile Stewardship Program shows promise of maintaining adequately high confidence for the indefinite future.

Nevertheless, the program is still developing, so its costs and risks are not known presently, and it is likely that their understanding will continue to evolve over the life of the program. This means that a dedicated Federal commitment will be necessary over the long haul if the program is to succeed.

Maintaining readiness to resume testing is a central and compelling ingredient of implementing a CTBT. This readiness provides a hedge against stewardship failure and against a treaty breakout by another nation. The period between a decision to resume testing and actual test execution could be a period of real or perceived vulnerability, and is consequently a period of extreme danger. That window of real or perceived vulnerability needs to be made as small as possible.

Implementation of a Comprehensive Test Ban Treaty would be a remarkable achievement that offers significant promise of strategic nuclear stability. It could be a critical milestone along the path of nuclear disarmament. But there are significant uncertainties in its consequences, in our ability to manage and respond to those consequences, and in the fidelity of assured compliance with the terms of the treaty. These uncertainties and their associated issues will be the subject of intense debate by the Senate as we move toward a policy decision that will define an appropriate balance between the treaty's costs, its risks, and its promised benefits.

STATEMENT OF BYRON L. DORGAN

Senator DOMENICI. Senator Dorgan.

Senator DORGAN. Mr. Chairman, I think this hearing is an excellent hearing. I appreciate your leadership and look forward to hearing our witnesses. I would simply say that I support the Comprehensive Test Ban Treaty. I would hope that we could see rather swift Senate ratification of that.

I do have a Commerce Committee hearing at the same time, so I will have to be in and out. Thank you so much.

STATEMENT OF FEDERICO PEÑA

Senator DOMENICI. Thank you, Senator.

Would you please proceed, Mr. Secretary. You know our time constraints and we know that you have a lot of things to do. Your remarks will be handled however you like. You have a written statement and it will be made a part of the record as if read. You may either give it or parcel it out, whichever you prefer.

Secretary PEÑA. Thank you very much, Mr. Chairman. Let me also salute you and congratulate you for having the foresight to have such an early hearing on such a very important matter. I also want to thank the members of the subcommittee who are here this afternoon.

Mr. Chairman, I do have a fuller set of remarks which I would like to formally submit for the record.

Senator DOMENICI. They will be made part of the record.

Secretary PEÑA. Let me, if I may, present some abbreviated remarks. I will try to follow the general guideline you gave in opening the hearing. But I believe there are some significant points that I do want to make and I would be very happy to try to answer whatever questions you may have.

STOCKPILE SAFETY AND RELIABILITY

Mr. Chairman, since becoming the Secretary of Energy, I have made the safety and reliability of our Nation's nuclear stockpile a top priority. In my confirmation hearing, I stated that I could not imagine any responsibility more serious than certifying to the President on an annual basis that our nuclear stockpile was safe and reliable.

Since my confirmation in March, I have visited each of the Department's three weapons laboratories and have personally engaged each of the weapons laboratory directors in discussions about the strength and adequacy of stockpile stewardship. I have also met with experts both within and outside of the Department and I am pleased to report: One, that there is strong consensus that stockpile stewardship is the right program to address the challenges of maintaining our nuclear deterrent without underground nuclear testing; two, that the program is properly sized and funded for the out-years; and, three, that with the President's six safeguards, we can enter into the Comprehensive Test Ban Treaty [CTBT] with confidence that the safety and reliability of our nuclear deterrent can be maintained.

ANNUAL STOCKPILE CERTIFICATION

These recent months of analysis and interagency review have allowed us to complete the technical assessments that form the basis for our second annual certification that the stockpile remains safe and reliable and that there is no need to return to underground nuclear testing at this time.

Secretary Cohen and I will soon make this certification to the President. As part of this process, I have personally spoken to each of the weapons laboratory directors and to the commander in chief of the Strategic Command to insure that they are confident in their assessment—and they are—of the safety and reliability of the stockpile.

The quest to end underground nuclear testing and to legislate a CTBT began decades ago with Presidents Eisenhower and Kennedy. With the end of the cold war, we finally have an opportunity to achieve this bipartisan goal.

The transmittal of the treaty by President Clinton to the Senate for its advice and consent to ratification last month represents the culmination of many years of effort on the part of the U.S. Government agencies, the national laboratories, and the Congress.

There continues to be overwhelming public support for such a treaty, and for good reason. This treaty provides a significant benefit to our national security. It will contribute to the prevention of nuclear proliferation and the process of further nuclear disarmament.

Even with these contributions, we recognize that the global community continues to face difficult security challenges. To meet the challenges, a credible nuclear deterrent, the foundation of our U.S. national security, must be maintained.

As the President has stated, the United States must and will retain strategic nuclear forces sufficient to deter any future hostile foreign leadership with access to strategic nuclear forces from acting against our vital interests.

In this regard, the President said, "I consider the maintenance of a safe and reliable nuclear stockpile to be a supreme national interest of the United States."

Mr. Chairman, it has been more than 5 years since our last underground test and, as the Secretary of Defense and I will soon certify to the President, the stockpile is both safe and reliable today. Our job now is to continue to maintain the safety and reliability of the deterrent under a CTBT. Why do we think we can meet this challenge and what are we doing to manage the risks?

TREATY SAFEGUARDS

In August 1995, when the President first announced that the United States would pursue a zero-yield CTBT, he declared that U.S. adherence would be predicated upon six safeguards. I am here because the Department of Energy plays a vital role in each of those six safeguards.

Let me briefly highlight those for you.

Safeguard A requires the conduct of a Science-Based Stockpile Stewardship Program. President Clinton directed the Department of Energy to develop stockpile stewardship more than 4 years ago, and he has repeatedly asked for the sustained bipartisan support of Congress for this program. We have made enormous strides in this program over the last several years.

I have visited our laboratories to see first hand the progress of the Stockpile Stewardship Program. I am pleased to report that it is working. We are successfully addressing several stockpile warhead issues by using a combination of analysis, new experimental data, archived test and manufacturing data, and, most importantly, the collective judgment of our weapon design laboratories. These successes, using the experimental and testing tools available today, provide confidence that the even more powerful computing and testing tools being developed now will allow us to solve future stockpile problems without nuclear testing.

Safeguard B requires the maintenance of modern nuclear laboratory facilities and programs in theoretical and exploratory nuclear technology. A number of activities being conducted as part of the Stockpile Stewardship Program are designed to help us carry out our responsibilities under this safeguard.

For example, in May, I participated in the groundbreaking ceremony for the national ignition facility at Lawrence Livermore National Laboratory. The NIF is designed to produce, for the first time in a laboratory setting, conditions of temperature and density of matter close to those that occur in the detonation of nuclear weapons. The ability to study the behavior of matter and energy under these conditions is key to understanding the basic physics of nuclear weapons and predicting their performance without underground nuclear testing.

Another central component of our program is the accelerated strategic computing initiative, called ASCI. It provides the leading-edge, high-end simulation capabilities needed to meet weapon assessment and certification requirements without nuclear testing. I believe that with the sustained, bipartisan support of the administration and this Congress, the new experimental facilities and programs will expand and enhance the scientific and engineering base for stockpile stewardship. In addition, they will assure that we can continue to attract and retain the high quality personnel needed to make the sound scientific and technical judgments on the safety and reliability of the stockpile in the absence of underground nuclear testing.

Safeguard C requires the maintenance of a basic capability to resume underground testing. We are meeting this requirement through a number of important activities at the Nevada test site, including the conduct of subcritical experiments. I have visited the Nevada test site. I want to thank Senator Reid for his hospitality in helping me through that visit in August because it has been over a decade since a Secretary of Energy last visited the Nevada test site.

While I was there, I spoke to the scientists who are responsible for the successful completion of our two subcritical experiments. These experiments, a key element of stockpile stewardship, will help us improve our basic knowledge of the properties of plutonium.

In addition, consistent with this safeguard, we are maintaining the capability at the test site to resume nuclear testing if directed by the President.

The President's inclusion of safeguards D and E recognizes the importance of continuing research and development in monitoring and verification to the success of the treaty. The Department of Energy CTBT research program is further developing the necessary core monitoring technologies to increase confidence in verifiability. The research program addresses all of the CTBT international monitoring system technology areas as well as technologies for on-site inspection and confidence building measures.

Safeguard F, the supreme national interest clause, specifies that if the President is informed by the Secretaries of Energy and Defense, advised by the Nuclear Weapons Council, the directors of the weapons laboratories, and the commander of the Strategic Command, that a high level of confidence in the safety or reliability of a weapon type critical to the nuclear deterrent could no longer be certified, the President, in consultation with the Congress, would be prepared to withdraw from the Comprehensive Test Ban Treaty in order to conduct whatever nuclear testing might be required.

To determine the overall safety and reliability of the stockpile, the President directed the establishment of a rigorous annual certification process. As I noted, we expect to complete the second of these annual certifications very soon.

Senator DOMENICI. Mr. Secretary, I am going to take a telephone call. You can proceed.

Senator Reid, would you chair while I am gone. I will be back shortly. It won't take me but 2 minutes.

Secretary PEÑA. Thank you, Mr. Chairman.

ANNUAL STOCKPILE CERTIFICATION

Mr. Chairman and members of the subcommittee, I was going to refer to a chart that I have here before us. But given the nature of the time for this hearing, perhaps I will not go through it in detail.

The purpose for presenting this chart to you—and I believe you have copies before you—is to give you a sense of the thoroughness and the reaffirmation of the process that we use in order to allow both the Secretary of Defense and the Secretary of Energy to certify to the President that, in fact, our weapons are safe and reliable.

ANNUAL CERTIFICATION

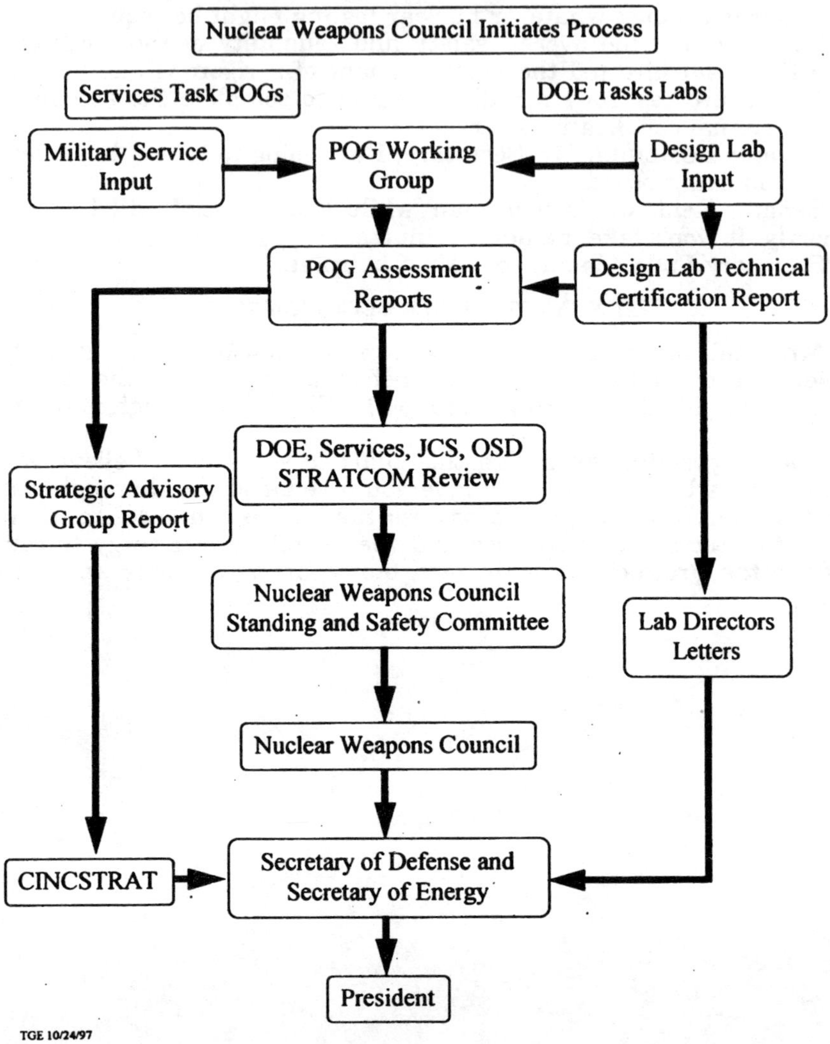

Let me just give you a quick summary to give you a sense of how we are able to make this certification with confidence.

We start at the top, with the Nuclear Weapons Council, which initiates the process. If you look at the chart, you will see that on the left-hand side we have DOD making all of its military inputs. The services task the project officers group and they give their input in terms of concerns they may have.

On the Department of Energy side, we have our laboratory directors who also input their advice.

The importance of the working group is that they make an assessment for each class of weapon and develop a report for each class of weapon. I have been shown these reports. They then go through DOE, the Joint Chiefs of Staff, the Office of the Secretary of Defense, and STRATCOM for review. From there they go to the Standing and Safety Committee of the Nuclear Weapons Council, then to the Nuclear Weapons Council, and then to me and to the Secretary of Defense upon which we decide whether we want to make the certification to the President.

The point that I want to make here is that, while we do this collaboratively between the Department of Defense and the Department of Energy, we also have independent reviews. For example, the commander in chief of the Strategic Command, General Habiger, has his own advisory group, former laboratory directors, and others who advise him in reviewing the strategic advisory group report.

Similarly, on the right side of the chart, in terms of DOE, I also get independent letters from each of the laboratory directors giving me their best judgment about the safety and reliability of the stockpile. Based on these independent reviews, the Secretary of Defense and the Secretary of Energy then jointly send a letter to the President indicating our confidence in the reliability and safety of the stockpile.

I wanted to review that for you to give you a sense of the thoroughness and the way in which we proceed. It is simply not a ratification of what others have suggested.

CLOSING REMARKS

In conclusion, Mr. Chairman, let me state that the President has made the Comprehensive Test Ban Treaty one of his highest national security priorities, and the President is committed to working with the Congress on stockpile stewardship. The administration's continuing support for stockpile stewardship underscores that our nuclear forces will continue to serve as a deterrent against aggression and coercion, a hedge against an uncertain future, a guarantee of our security commitments to our allies, and a discouragement to those who would contemplate developing or otherwise acquiring their own nuclear weapons.

When the President made the United States the first signatory of the Comprehensive Test Ban Treaty at the U.N. General Assembly last year, he demonstrated that the United States is committed to being a leader in this area. He signed the treaty with the very same pen that President Kennedy used because he thought it was important to show that we were passing the torch.

We are passing that very same torch with a new generation of engineers who will be working with our current engineers and scientists who will prepare themselves for the future. It is because we believe that this treaty is fundamentally in the national security interest of the United States that we also ask for your support.

Millions of Americans, perhaps more than ever before, long for the peace of mind that comes with knowing that our world is safe from either accidental or intentional nuclear disaster. By constraining nuclear and nonnuclear weapons States from developing more advanced weapon types, the treaty serves our nonproliferation and disarmament goals and moves us all closer to achieving this peace of mind.

Mr. Chairman, thank you very much for allowing me to make my opening statement. I am very pleased now to respond to any questions from you or Senator Reid.

[The statement follows:]

PREPARED STATEMENT OF SECRETARY FEDERICO PEÑA

Good afternoon Mr. Chairman and members of the Subcommittee. It is a pleasure to appear before you this afternoon to discuss the Comprehensive Test Ban Treaty (CTBT) and how the Department of Energy's Stockpile Stewardship program allows us to maintain the safety and reliability of our nation's nuclear stockpile.

Since becoming the Secretary of Energy, I have made the safety and reliability of our nation's nuclear stockpile a top priority. In my confirmation hearing, I stated that I cannot imagine any responsibility more serious than certifying to the President on an annual basis whether or not our nuclear stockpile is both safe and reliable.

Since my confirmation in March, I have visited each of the Department's three weapons laboratories, and have personally engaged each of the weapons laboratory directors in discussions about the strength and adequacy of Stockpile Stewardship. I have also met with other experts both within and outside of the Department, and I am pleased to report that there is a strong consensus that Stockpile Stewardship is the right program to address the challenges of maintaining our nuclear deterrent without underground nuclear testing; that the program is properly sized and funded for the outyears; and that, with the President's six safeguards, we can enter into the Comprehensive Test Ban Treaty with confidence that the safety and reliability of our nuclear deterrent can be maintained.

These recent months of analysis and interagency review have also allowed us to complete the technical assessments that form the basis for our second annual certification that the stockpile remains safe and reliable. I expect that Secretary Cohen and I will soon certify to the President that the stockpile is safe and reliable and that there is no need to resume underground nuclear testing at this time. As part of this certification process, I have spoken to each of the weapons laboratory directors, and to the Commander-in-Chief of Strategic Command to ensure that they are confident in their assessment—and they are—of the safety and reliability of the stockpile.

The quest to end all nuclear weapons test explosions began decades ago with Presidents Eisenhower and Kennedy. With the end of the Cold War, we finally have the opportunity to achieve this bipartisan goal.

The transmittal of the Treaty by President Clinton to the Senate for its advice and consent to ratification last month represents the culmination of many years of effort on the part of United States government agencies, the National Laboratories, and the Congress. There continues to be overwhelming public support for such a treaty, and for good reason. This treaty provides a significant benefit to the national security of the United States. It will contribute to the prevention of nuclear proliferation and the process of further nuclear disarmament.

We recognize that the global community continues to face difficult security challenges. To meet the challenges, a credible nuclear deterrent—the foundation of U.S. national security—must be maintained. As the President has stated, "the United States must and will retain strategic nuclear forces sufficient to deter any future hostile foreign leadership with access to strategic nuclear forces from acting against our vital interests * * * in this regard * * * I consider the maintenance of a safe and reliable nuclear stockpile to be a supreme national interest of the United States."

It has been more than five years since our last underground test and, as Secretary Cohen and I will soon certify to the President, the stockpile is both safe and reliable today. Our job now is to continue to maintain the safety and reliability of the deterrent under a CTBT. Why do we think we can meet this challenge, and what are we doing to manage the risks?

In August of 1995, when President Clinton first announced that the United States would pursue a zero-yield CTBT, he declared that U.S. adherence to a CTBT would be predicated upon six safeguards:

(A) The conduct of a Science-Based Stockpile Stewardship program—for which there must be sustained bipartisan support from Congress—to ensure a high level of confidence in the safety and reliability of our nuclear weapons stockpile;

(B) The maintenance of modern nuclear laboratory facilities and programs in theoretical and exploratory nuclear technology;

(C) The maintenance of a basic capability to resume nuclear test activities prohibited by the CTBT should the United States cease to be bound to adhere to the Treaty;

(D) A continued comprehensive research and development program for treaty verification and monitoring operations;

(E) The continued development of a broad range of intelligence gathering and analytical capabilities; and

(F) The understanding that if the President is informed by the Secretaries of Defense and Energy as advised by the Nuclear Weapons Council, the Directors of the nuclear weapons laboratories, and Commander of U.S. Strategic Command that a high level of confidence in the safety and reliability of a nuclear weapon type which the two secretaries consider critical to our nuclear deterrent could no longer be certified, the President, in consultation with the Congress, would be prepared to withdraw from CTBT under the supreme national interest clause.

I am here today because the Department of Energy plays a vital role in each of these six safeguards. And I am here because I consider the stewardship of our nation's nuclear stockpile to be my highest responsibility. I have emphasized the significance of this responsibility with each of the directors of our nuclear weapons laboratories and I will continue to stress the Department's responsibility to uphold the six safeguards that the President outlined. I would now like to briefly highlight our role in each of these six safeguards.

SAFEGUARD A

Safeguard A requires the conduct of a Science-Based Stockpile Stewardship program. President Clinton directed the Department of Energy to develop this program more than four years ago. We have made enormous strides in this program over the last several years. The program has been designed to combine laboratory experimentation with advanced computations in lieu of underground nuclear testing to ensure high confidence in the safety and reliability of the stockpile.

I have visited our three nuclear weapons laboratories to see firsthand the progress of the Stockpile Stewardship program. I am pleased to report that Stockpile Stewardship is working. We are successfully addressing several stockpile warhead issues by using a combination of analysis, new experimental data, archived test and manufacturing data, and most importantly, the collective judgment of our weapon design laboratories. These successes, using the experimental and testing tools available today, provides confidence that those even more powerful computing and testing tools being developed now will allow us to solve future stockpile problems without nuclear testing.

Our stewardship program is also designed so that the day-to-day needs of the stockpile are met in a cost efficient and environmentally responsible manner. The production plants at Savannah River, Pantex, Kansas City, and Oak Ridge are producing critical limited life components, like tritium reservoirs, and making the necessary repairs to support the enduring nuclear weapons stockpile.

SAFEGUARD B

Safeguard B requires the maintenance of modern nuclear laboratory facilities and programs in theoretical and exploratory nuclear technology. A number of activities being conducted as part of the Stockpile Stewardship program are designed to help us carry out our responsibilities under this safeguard. In May, I participated in the groundbreaking ceremony for the National Ignition Facility at Lawrence Livermore National Laboratory. NIF is designed to produce, for the first time in a laboratory setting, conditions of temperature and density of matter close to those that occur in the detonation of nuclear weapons. The ability to study the behavior of matter and energy under these conditions is key to understanding the basic physics of nuclear weapons and predicting their performance without underground nuclear testing.

Another central component of our program is the Accelerated Strategic Computing Initiative. ASCI provides the leading-edge, high-end simulation capabilities needed to meet weapon assessment and certification requirements without nuclear testing. The national laboratories are focused on providing the application codes and related science needed to address weapon safety, reliability, and performance. They are also developing improved tools and methodologies to utilize this unprecedented volume of data.

Even at this early stage in their development, advanced ASCI codes are providing unprecedented capabilities to our weapons program. For example, we have reduced the time it takes to complete one simulation from 74 days to 7 hours. We are not only doing the same things faster, we are performing calculations and simulations that we once only imagined possible.

I believe that with the sustained, bipartisan support of the Administration and the Congress, the new experimental facilities and programs will expand and enhance the scientific and engineering base for Stockpile Stewardship, and assure that we can continue to attract and retain the high quality personnel needed to make the sound scientific and technical judgments on the safety and reliability of the stockpile in the absence of underground nuclear testing.

SAFEGUARD C

Safeguard C requires the maintenance of a basic capability to resume underground testing. We are meeting this requirement through a number of important activities at the Nevada Test Site, including the conduct of subcritical experiments. I visited the Nevada Test Site in August and spoke to the scientists responsible for the successful completion of our subcritical experiments. These experiments—a key element of Stockpile Stewardship—will help us improve our basic knowledge of the properties of plutonium. In addition, consistent with this safeguard, we are maintaining the capability at the Test Site to resume nuclear testing, if directed by the President.

My visit in August is the first that a Secretary of Energy has made to the Test Site in more than a decade. I was impressed by the dedication and the talent of the scientists and engineers who are responsible for conducting the subcritical experiments.

SAFEGUARDS D AND E

The President's inclusion of Safeguards D and E recognizes the importance of continuing research and development in monitoring and verification to the success of the Treaty. The Department of Energy's CTBT research program is further developing the necessary core monitoring technologies to increase confidence in verifiability. The research program addresses all of the CTBT International Monitoring System (IMS) technology areas—seismic, infrasound, radionuclide, and hydroacoustic—as well as technologies for on-site inspection and confidence building measures. For example, to provide for CTBT radionuclide regional monitoring, we have developed an automated ultra-sensitive near real-time radionuclide detection and analysis system. These technologies meet IMS specifications, and are available commercially.

In addition, Department of Energy research programs are helping to improve U.S. National Technical Means related to CTBT monitoring. For example, the Department is also conducting research and development for satellite-based detection systems.

SAFEGUARD F

Safeguard F specifies that if the President is informed by the Secretaries of Energy and Defense, advised by the Nuclear Weapons Council, the directors of the weapons laboratories, and the Commander-in-Chief of Strategic Command that a high-level of confidence in the safety or reliability of a weapon type critical to the nuclear deterrent could no longer be certified, the President, in consultation with the Congress, would be prepared to withdraw from the CTBT under the Supreme National Interest Clause in order to conduct whatever nuclear testing might be required.

To determine the overall safety and reliability of the stockpile, the President directed the establishment of a rigorous, annual certification process. As I noted, we expect to complete the second of these annual certifications soon. I would like to take a moment to explain how this process works. As you can see, it is a comprehensive and thorough procedure.

The certification process requires that the weapons design laboratories and the Department of Defense review all weapons types—both active and inactive. From this review, the laboratory directors, the Nuclear Weapons Council, and the Commander-in-Chief of Strategic Command each independently advise the Secretaries of Energy and Defense on the results. Based upon these results, we determine whether or not to certify to the President that there is no need to return to underground nuclear testing.

The rigor and thoroughness of this procedure ensures that, from the level of the technicians working with the weapons on a day-to-day basis, to the designers who know the inner workings of the weapons, to Secretary Cohen and myself, every level of authority is appropriately informed of and accountable for the safety and reliability of the weapons stockpile.

And let me stress that if I am advised by the nuclear weapons laboratory directors that there is a problem with the stockpile that is critical to our nuclear deterrent and that we are unable to correct without returning to underground nuclear testing, I will not hesitate to advise the President of such.

CONCLUSION

President Clinton has made the CTBT one of his highest national security priorities and is committed to working with the Congress on the Stockpile Stewardship program. At the same time, the Administration's continuing support for Stockpile Stewardship underscores that our nuclear forces will continue to serve as a deterrent against aggression and coercion, a hedge against an uncertain future, a guarantee of our security commitment to allies, and a discouragement to those who would contemplate developing or otherwise acquiring their own nuclear weapons.

When President Clinton made the United States the first signatory of the Comprehensive Test Ban Treaty at the United Nations General Assembly last year, he demonstrated that the United States is committed to being the leader in this arena. He signed the Treaty with the very same pen that President Kennedy used to bring the Limited Test Ban Treaty to life. A symbolic gesture, but a meaningful one. The gesture symbolized the passing of a torch from one generation to the next.

At our weapons laboratories right now, the torch is being passed. A generation of scientists and engineers who created the awesome power behind the mushroom cloud are passing the torch to a generation of scientists and engineers, who may never know its shadow. To this new generation of scientists and engineers, the CTBT, and the stewardship program that underpins it, is our commitment to the national security that they work so very hard every day to protect.

It is because we believe that this Treaty is fundamentally in the national security interest of the United States that we ask your support. Millions of Americans, perhaps more than ever before, long for the peace of mind that comes with knowing that our world is safe from either accidental or intentional nuclear disaster. By constraining not only nuclear weapons development by non-nuclear weapons states, but also the development of more advanced weapon types by nuclear weapon states, the Treaty serves our nonproliferation and disarmament goals, and moves us closer to achieving this peace of mind.

ANNUAL CERTIFICATION

Senator DOMENICI. Senator Reid, do you have any questions?

Senator REID. Yes, thank you.

Mr. Secretary, with the certification process there is no congressional involvement other than appropriating the necessary money. Is that true?

Secretary PEÑA. That's correct, Senator.

Senator REID. How much time is there from beginning to end of the certification process?

Secretary PEÑA. The first certification—and I must speak from what I have been informed since it was conducted by my predecessor, then Acting Secretary Curtis—took at least 1 year. It was the first time that the annual certification had occurred. In fact, it took a little over 1 year.

Since that time, we have made very significant progress in doing the second certification. And, in fact, as respects the process of the second certification, the Nuclear Weapons Council has already acted on the information provided to it. It has now been transmitted to both myself and the Secretary of Defense and we hope very soon to make the final judgment about the second annual certification.

FUNDING FOR STOCKPILE STEWARDSHIP PROGRAM

Senator REID. It is my understanding that the administration believes the stockpile can be maintained without testing as we have known it for about $4.5 billion a year for the next 10 years. So that is $4.5 billion times 10.

Is that something that you agree with?

Secretary PEÑA. I do, Senator. If I could just amplify that a bit, as you know, when the Stockpile Stewardship Program was first designed, it was contemplated that about $4 billion per year would be needed.

We have observed in the last several years of the program that additional needs were presented to the team responsible for the Stockpile Stewardship Program and also that some additional issues had been funded in previous years—for example, emergency preparedness—which were not directly related to stockpile stewardship.

For those and other reasons, we have now agreed that for fiscal year 1999 we will formally submit to the Congress an amount of $4.5 billion for stockpile stewardship. It will then serve as the baseline for the out-years. And we will formally submit that early next year as part of our formal budget presentation to the Congress.

Senator REID. As I think you have indicated and I want to make sure this is right, the $4.5 billion does cover all the known requirements for maintaining a safe and reliable stockpile, is that right?

Secretary PEÑA. That's correct, Senator.

Senator REID. Also, your certifying is dependent on information you get from our laboratories and other such information, is that not true?

Secretary PEÑA. From a number of sources, that's correct: Our laboratories, the Nuclear Weapons Council, the STRATCOM, and then whatever questions and information I gather when I visit the labs, when I visit the test site, and other forms of information.

Senator REID. There is no fat in this $4.5 billion, then? This is what the administration is determined is the amount of money needed to certify safety and reliability for the stockpile?

Secretary PEÑA. That's correct, Senator. This is a very precise budget. We have spent many, many hours, not only with our laboratory directors but with obviously the DOE team, with the Department of Defense, with OMB and others to arrive at the $4.5 billion amount.

Senator REID. The last question I would ask orally is this, and I would ask permission to submit some other questions in writing. We, as appropriators, need to get $4.5 billion for you to certify safety and reliability of this arsenal. This is not a number that you have given us that has fat in it so that we can come back with $4.1 billion and you will be able to do your job. So, it is $4.5 billion to do your job, then, and nothing less. Is that true?

Secretary PEÑA. That's correct, Senator.

Senator REID. Thank you, Mr. Chairman.

IMPORTANCE OF STOCKPILE STEWARDSHIP PROGRAM

Senator DOMENICI. Thank you very much, Senator.

Mr. Secretary and other members of the administration who are here as proponents of the treaty, I assume you know all of this. But I just wanted to make sure that I told you this.

If you want to hear at least one serious, lengthy discussion against the treaty, you all ought to get the testimony of Dr. Jim Schlesinger who testified before the Committee on Governmental Affairs, which has jurisdiction over much of this on the authorizing side.

Incidentally, an interesting observation was made by Dr. Schlesinger for some of you who are more technical than I and perhaps more technical than the Secretary. He said, "Don't misunderstand me. Even if we were permitted to do nuclear testing, if you asked me for my recommendation, I would also say you ought to also have stockpile stewardship anyway."

So it is interesting, his observation of what this program will do.

My second observation, Mr. Secretary—and these are among the early hearings, so I think we ought to put some of these issues out—is clearly Dr. Schlesinger's arguments and the arguments that many will make on the same side do not concern themselves with the next 4 years or even the next 10 years. They are talking about 15, 20, and 25 years out.

I am not so sure that I want to say it is that far out. But, nonetheless, the point of it is, the concern is that we are locked into the treaty in perpetuity short of our pulling ourselves out. I guess from the standpoint of some experts, the fact that you could maintain a valid stockpile without testing at some time is an issue that will find itself in these discussions on this treaty without any question.

I want to just ask about two issues.

CTBT TREATY OBLIGATIONS AND PROHIBITION

I understand that the treaty obligations only prohibit the conducting of nuclear explosions. I do not believe that the CTBT is a nuclear disarmament treaty.

I believe you said that. But would you agree with that?

Secretary PEÑA. Senator, if I understand the nature of the question, you are correct. What is prohibited is nuclear explosions either for military purposes or peaceful purposes. However, there are other forms of energy releases which are permitted under the CTBT and there is a history in the negotiations which allow certain things. For example, the national ignition facility [NIF] is accepted as being consistent with the Comprehensive Test Ban Treaty.

Senator DOMENICI. I am going to get to another question in 1 minute. But I was making an observation that the treaty only prohibits the conduct of nuclear explosions. I believe that it is not a nuclear disarmament treaty. Is that correct?

Secretary PEÑA. That is correct, Senator. I misunderstood your question.

Senator DOMENICI. I think the President, I note in sending this treaty up, was very clear. There are a lot of ways this treaty has been expressed, even by the President in various speeches, which we have noted. But when he sent it up, he said that the language does not imply that the treaty prohibits the development of new types of nuclear weapons or the improvement of existing weapons. It does recognize that the treaty will have the effect of constraining in some way such activities.

NEW OR MODIFIED WEAPON DESIGN NEEDS

Now I want to ask you this question. Does the treaty take away the rights of any country, including ours, to build or design new nuclear weapons or to modify existing nuclear weapons?

Secretary PEÑA. No, sir.

Senator DOMENICI. Would the treaty, if it were ratified, have any relevance to the recent decision to modify the B–61 bomb to have an earth penetrating capability?

Secretary PEÑA. We believe it does not, Senator.

Senator DOMENICI. The effectiveness of this treaty in constraining the development of nuclear weapons by rogue States is a discussion piece. Many are talking about what is the impact on the potential of rogue States having nuclear bombs.

Now from what I understand, the United States did not need a test for one of the designs used in World War II, and the earliest U.S. weapons were designed with computer tools far less sophisticated than any modern personal computer of today.

Now I am not a historian, but I am told that is the case. Perhaps Dr. Smith can confirm that when he takes the witness stand.

PROLIFERATION OF NUCLEAR WEAPONS

In the Governmental Affairs hearing on Monday, both Secretary Schlesinger and Dr. Barker questioned whether the CTBT would limit actions of rogue States, like Iraq, Iran, Libya, or North Korea, to develop their own weapons or to use testing that suited their purposes.

Now what assurances do we have that the existence of this new treaty will constrain development of nuclear capabilities by a rogue nation and, thus, effectively curb proliferation of nuclear weapons?

Secretary PEÑA. Senator, that is a very good question. By the way, let me say that I have had two conversations with Dr. Schlesinger about these matters. So we have, I think, had a very constructive discussion about it.

We strongly believe that the Comprehensive Test Ban Treaty, in the way that it has verifiability provisions, in the way that it puts forth a rather extensive monitoring system throughout the globe, in the way in which it allows information to be presented to the Executive Council by which a country which allegedly has conducted a test inconsistent with the treaty, effectively allows us to deter nations from conducting the types of tests that are necessary to develop sophisticated nuclear weapons.

I believe that the experts who will talk to you in a classified setting will perhaps share that there may be some very basic types of weapons that may not need the kind of testing that we are concerned about. But for very sophisticated weapons, we believe no country can develop those unless they have the ability to do underground testing.

Because this treaty, if ratified and in effect by the nations of the world, would prohibit those kinds of tests, we believe that effectively it prevents and deters and certainly discourages other countries from even beginning to consider the kind of testing necessary for the development of very sophisticated nuclear weapons. In that sense, it is a very effective deterrent to the proliferation of nuclear weapons throughout the world.

Senator DOMENICI. I believe, Senator Reid, you asked whether or not there was anything that the Congress had to do other than to ratify this treaty as it pertains to this treaty.

Senator REID. And appropriate the money.

Senator DOMENICI. And appropriate the money, yes. I might say, obviously, the Senator is correct and the response that you gave is correct.

ENABLING LEGISLATION FOR THE CTBT

But it does seem that in order to make sure that this treaty is supported, we may have to get enabling legislation passed that creates some assurances with reference to how we are going to conduct ourselves with reference to supporting what this treaty needs. I assume you are looking at some possible enabling legislation and you will be open to discussing that with various committees?

Secretary PEÑA. That's correct, Mr. Chairman. There are a number of enabling pieces of legislation which would be, I think, appropriate for final passage.

But if I might, I believe the question that Senator Reid asked me was particularly about this process. He asked, as I walked through this chart, if the Congress was particularly involved in this process [indicating], and I answered no as respect to this process.

But, obviously, the Congress is involved in many other ways.

Senator DOMENICI. I was out of the room and returned in the middle of that discussion. I apologize for my misinterpretation. But I think essentially we understand each other.

Before I move on to some other witnesses, I want to make a couple of comments to you.

RESPONSIBILITIES OF DOE

Mr. Secretary, when you were assigned, designated by the President to be the Secretary of Energy, we had some rather lengthy meetings. I believe my best advice was that the success of the Department of Energy for any prolonged period of time here in the Congress would probably rely almost exclusively on how you conducted yourself with reference to that part of the Department of Energy that has to do with maintaining the nuclear arsenal.

I believe I suggested to you that the most questionable aspects about the Department of Energy among many Senators was whether or not it would appropriately handle, year by year, the requirements of maintaining this nuclear arsenal.

I was very pleased that you listened attentively and that on a couple of occasions thereafter you concurred. I want to compliment you.

This is not to say that you don't have many other powerful functions in the Department. I think when you have one of the powerful hands with reference to nuclear bombs and nuclear weapons maintenance, I assume you end up thinking it is a very important part of your mission.

I do want to compliment you on how much time you have designated to it and how diligently you have gone about learning the job and, equally as important thus far, the kind of people you are surrounding yourself with. I think we talked about that, too.

We cannot have people with three or four missions in life talking about maintaining the stockpile. They have to be preoccupied with and worried about it and it has to be very predominant in their thinking.

While we have not been able to approve all of your designees, I think we are going to. We have six of them waiting up here.

Secretary PEÑA. Last night, Senator, five were approved.

Senator DOMENICI. And I think the sixth is going to be approved now.

So thank you very much. You don't have to stay around for the rest of the hearing. I know that you have much to do.

We are going to proceed with the next panel.

Secretary PEÑA. Thank you very much, Mr. Chairman.

Thank you, Senator Reid.

Senator DOMENICI. Thank you.

Senator REID. Thank you, Mr. Secretary.

DEPARTMENT OF DEFENSE

STATEMENT OF FRANKLIN C. MILLER, ACTING ASSISTANT SECRETARY OF DEFENSE FOR INTERNATIONAL SECURITY POLICY

Senator DOMENICI. Our next panel is made up of Vic Reis, Dr. Smith, and Mr. Miller. Whether it is the Defense Department supporting the DOE nuclear programs or the DOE supporting Defense, in any event, you are all friends today.

Dr. REIS. Yes; we are all friends today—and it is really more than just today, sir.

Senator DOMENICI. We will begin the second panel now. We will have questions about two issues that are going to require some closed sessions which we will do afterwards. We will just ask you to go with us to the closed session room. It won't take us very long.

We are going to start now with Mr. Miller. Dr. Smith, you should go second. Dr. Reis, if you don't mind, you will go third.

First, I want Mr. Miller to review the current U.S. nuclear weapons requirements. Then I want you to explain how those might change, what our stockpile will be if Russia ratifies START II, whether the tritium reserve requirements might change and the status of dealerting proposals, and consideration of changes in the makeup of the TRIAD.

I think you are aware of that. Then, when I get to Dr. Smith, I will tell you what I am hopeful you will present to us.

Mr. Miller.

STATEMENT OF FRANKLIN C. MILLER

Mr. MILLER. Thank you, Senator Domenici, Senator Reid.

I am honored to have this opportunity to appear before you to discuss the confidence in the safety and reliability of our stockpile without nuclear explosive tests.

With your permission, Mr. Chairman, I will begin with a brief historical perspective.

Since the end of the Second World War, U.S. nuclear weapons have deterred major aggression threatening the United States and our allies. It was that deterrent against the backdrop of the cold war which broke the historic and periodic pattern of total conventional war. It is a remarkable fact that, for almost one-half century, the United States and its allies faced the U.S.S.R. and its coerced auxiliaries armed to the greatest extent which huge sacrifice would afford and yet did not fight a large-scale war.

We successfully persevered long enough to allow Soviet communism to collapse of its own internal weaknesses.

Some had argued that the danger of nuclear weapons was so great that the risk of possessing them outweighed the benefits. But I don't think we agree. Nuclear deterrence helped buy us time, time for democracy and diplomacy to contain communism, time for the internal forces of upheaval and decay to rend the Soviet Union and the Warsaw Pact and bring about the end of the cold war. I don't think anybody doubts that our nuclear deterrent played an important role in all of this.

But the cold war is now over and the U.S. nuclear posture reflects this. I think history will make clear that that posture and our policy anticipated this historic development.

Nuclear deterrence requirements and the plans designed to implement them are the result of an intense, collaborative process between the Office of the Secretary of Defense, the joint staff, and the U.S. Strategic Command.

Working from broad national guidance, my staff, the joint staff, and the Strategic Command staff develop the targeting requirements which underpin U.S. nuclear deterrence policy. The type of delivery vehicles and the type of warheads carried by those delivery vehicles are derived directly from those targeting requirements.

The Navy and the Air Force then assume primary responsibility for the health and safety of the delivery systems, while my colleagues, Dr. Smith and Dr. Reis, assume primary responsibility for the health and safety of the nuclear stockpile itself.

STOCKPILE REDUCTIONS

As you point out, Senator Domenici, we are engaged in an arms control process. Over the past 10 years, but particularly since the end of the cold war, we have significantly reduced our nuclear weapons arsenal. We have done so on the basis of an analysis, a careful analysis, of the changes in the world and the consequent changes that our deterrence posture requires.

We have determined that many categories of weapons are no longer needed and we eliminated those categories.

All of this does not mean that nuclear weapons have no role in our future deterrent posture, in our future national security posture. In 1994, the administration's nuclear posture review reaffirmed the role of nuclear deterrence in our national security policy. But while we continue to explore the new possibilities for increased stability and future arms reduction treaties, we also plan to deploy a TRIAD of strategic nuclear delivery systems and a very limited arsenal of nonstrategic nuclear forces, insuring a survivable and effective deterrent force.

START I AND FUTURE FORCE LEVELS

Our current policy, in fact, the law of the land as mandated by the Congress, is that we maintain our forces at START I levels until START II is ratified by the Russian Duma and enters into force. At that point, we will proceed down to 3,500 to 3,000 nuclear warheads. But we will maintain a TRIAD.

We are examining, as the committee, knows, the START III requirements. We have worked a basic framework with the Russian government at Helsinki this spring, and that would further reduce strategic nuclear warheads to an active arsenal of between 2,000 and 2,500 weapons. Obviously and clearly, the requirements that we have for tritium will shrink, depending on the entry into force of START II and the successful negotiation and entry into force of START III.

But our current policy, again, as mandated by law, is to maintain START I levels until the Duma ratifies START II. Our policy is that we will not begin active negotiations of START III until the Duma ratifies START II.

The CTBT is an important element of our approach to national security in the post-cold war world. The United States took a leading role in the creation of the treaty. President Clinton was the first head of State to sign it and we look forward in the near future to receiving the Senate's advice and consent to the treaty.

KEY CTBT PRINCIPLES

The treaty is in the national security interests of the United States and it will constrain nuclear and nonnuclear weapons States from developing more advanced weapons capabilities. Nevertheless, under the CTBT, certain key principles will remain unchanged. Because nuclear weapons will continue to play a role in our national security strategy, the deterrent must remain credible.

The warheads and the systems that carry them must be safe, reliable, and effective, and the quality, reliability, and effectiveness of our forces, including command, control, and communications links and the people who operate them, are among our top priorities in the Department of Defense.

The safeguards which Secretary Peña alluded to and discussed, in fact, are structured to maintain our nuclear stockpile and insure our continued security under the CTBT.

In the interest of brevity, Mr. Chairman, I will not go through all of the safeguards because Secretary Peña spoke to them. Of course, safeguard A does mandate the establishment of a science-based Stockpile Stewardship Program which is absolutely essential to the safety and reliability of the stockpile under the CTBT.

Under the Stockpile Management Program, under the Stewardship Program, we may, in fact, in the future have to modify nuclear weapons and their delivery systems as, in the future, parts reach the end of their design life. These modifications are not prohibited by the CTBT. In fact, only nuclear weapon test explosions are prohibited.

While there is no current need to produce nuclear warhead designs, administration policy requires that the Department of Energy maintain that capability to respond to potential future requirements.

DOE must maintain the capability to refabricate and certify weapons types in the enduring stockpile.

TRITIUM SUPPLY

Mr. Chairman, you mentioned tritium. We in the Department of Defense are particularly interested in assuring the continuity of the tritium supply and we await with great anticipation a decision from the Department of Energy in the near future on its preferred approach to insuring the tritium production supply.

I will not discuss safeguard F as that has already been discussed by Secretary Peña.

VERIFICATION OF TREATY VIOLATIONS

Another CTBT matter of extreme importance is the verifiability of the treaty. We recognize that there are enormous monitoring challenges presented by the treaty. It is wider in its scope than those imposed by any previous nuclear test related treaty. But we believe that our existing and future programs will provide us the capability to do so.

There are, of course, conceivable CTBT evasion scenarios. But the administration believes the treaty is effectively verifiable because of the wide range of resources that we have. We have the means to assess whether the treaty is deterring the conduct of nuclear explosions and we believe that, in terms of numbers and yields of tests, that we would know if any nation were carrying out actions which could undermine U.S. security interests.

PREPARED STATEMENT

The administration's judgment that the CTBT is effectively verifiable also reflects the belief that U.S. nuclear deterrence would not be undermined by the numbers and yields of possible nuclear tests that the United States might fail to detect under the treaty.

Mr. Chairman, this concludes my prepared statement.

[The statement follows:]

PREPARED STATEMENT OF FRANKLIN C. MILLER

Mr. Chairman and members of the Subcommittee, I am honored to have this opportunity to appear before you today as this committee considers the important question of how the United States will ensure continued confidence in the safety and reliability of our nuclear stockpile without nuclear explosive tests.

With the Chairman's permission, I will begin by providing a brief historical perspective. Since the end of World War II, U.S. nuclear weapons have deterred major aggression threatening the U.S. and its allies. It was the U.S. nuclear deterrent which, against the backdrop of the Cold War, broke the historic and periodic pattern of total conventional war. It is a remarkable fact that for almost half a century, the U.S. and its allies faced the U.S.S.R. and its coerced auxiliaries, armed to the greatest extent huge sacrifice would afford, and yet did not fight a large-scale war. We successfully persevered long enough to allow Soviet Communism to collapse of its own internal weakness.

Some argued that the danger of a nuclear war was so great that the risk of possessing these weapons far outweighed their benefits. I do not agree. Nuclear deterrence helped buy us time, time for democracy and diplomacy to contain Communism; time for internal forces of upheaval and decay to rend the Soviet Union and the Warsaw Pact and bring about the end of the Cold War. Can anyone really doubt that our nuclear forces played an important role in this? But the Cold War is over now and the U.S. nuclear posture reflects this. Indeed, history will make clear that U.S. nuclear policy and posture anticipated this historic development.

Nuclear deterrence requirements—and the plans designed to implement them—are the result of an intense collaborative process between the Office of the Secretary of Defense, the Joint Staff, and the U.S. Strategic Command. Working from broad national guidance, my staff, the Joint Staff, and the STRATCOM staff develop the targeting requirements which underpin U.S. nuclear deterrence policy. The type of delivery vehicles and the type of warheads carried by those delivery vehicles are derived directly from those targeting requirements. The Navy and the Air Force then assume primary responsibility for the health and safety of the delivery systems, while my colleagues, Dr. Smith and Dr. Reis assume primary responsibility for the health and safety of the nuclear stockpile itself.

Over the past 10 years, but particularly since the last year of the Cold War, we have significantly reduced our nuclear weapons arsenal. We have done so based on careful examination of the changes in the world, and the consequent changes in our deterrence requirements. We determined that many categories of nuclear weapons were non-essential to our national security and have taken them out of the arsenal and eliminated them. We halted nuclear weapons systems development programs. But all of this does not mean that nuclear weapons have no role in our current or future security posture. In September 1994, the Administration's Nuclear Posture Review reaffirmed the importance of nuclear deterrence. The NPR recognized that the strategic environment has been important role in this? But the Cold War is over now and the U.S. nuclear posture reflects this. Indeed, history will make clear that U.S. nuclear policy and posture anticipated this historic development.

Nuclear deterrence requirements—and the plans designed to implement them—are the result of an intense collaborative process between the Office of the Secretary of Defense, the Joint Staff, and the U.S. Strategic Command. Working from broad national guidance, my staff, the Joint Staff, and the STRATCOM staff develop the targeting requirements which underpin U.S. nuclear deterrence policy. The type of delivery vehicles and the type of warheads carried by those delivery vehicles are derived directly from those targeting requirements. The Navy and the Air Force then assume primary responsibility for the health and safety of the delivery systems, while my colleagues, Dr. Smith and Dr. Reis assume primary responsibility for the health and safety of the nuclear stockpile itself.

Over the past 10 years, but particularly since the last year of the Cold War, we have significantly reduced our nuclear weapons arsenal. We have done so based on careful examination of the changes in the world, and the consequent changes in our deterrence requirements. We determined that many categories of nuclear weapons were non-essential to our national security and have taken them out of the arsenal and eliminated them. We halted nuclear weapons systems development programs. But all of this does not mean that nuclear weapons have no role in our current or future security posture. In September 1994, the Administration's Nuclear Posture Review reaffirmed the importance of nuclear deterrence. The NPR recognized that the strategic environment has been transformed. Conventional forces have assumed a larger share of our security posture. Nonetheless, nuclear weapons continue to play a critical role in deterring aggression against the U.S., our forces and our allies. While we continue to explore new possibilities for increased stability and future arms reduction treaties, we also plan to continue to deploy a triad of strategic nuclear delivery systems, and a very limited arsenal of non-strategic nuclear forces, ensuring a survivable and effective deterrent force.

The positive changes in the international environment are far from irreversible. And there are a range of new potential threats. One cannot survey the list of rogue states with potential WMD programs and conclude otherwise. The knowledge that the U.S. has a powerful and ready nuclear capability is, I believe, a significant deterrent to proliferators to even contemplate the use of WMD.

The CTBT is an important element of the Administration's approach to nuclear security in the post-Cold War world. The United States took a leading role in the creation of this treaty. President Clinton was the first head of state to sign it and we look forward in the near future to receiving the Senate's advice and consent to the Treaty. The Treaty is in the national security interests of the United States. It will constrain nuclear and non-nuclear weapons states from developing more advanced nuclear weapons capabilities.

Nevertheless, under a CTBT, certain key principles will remain unchanged. Because nuclear weapons will continue to play a role in our national security strategy for the foreseeable future, the Nation's nuclear deterrent must remain credible. Weapons systems and their warheads must be safe, reliable and effective. The quality, reliability, and effectiveness of our forces, including the command, control, and communications system, and the people who operate them are among our top priorities in the Department of Defense.

Under our national security strategy requiring a nuclear deterrent, the Administration's CTBT safeguards are structured to maintain our nuclear stockpile and ensure our continued security under a CTBT.

Safeguard A mandated the establishment of a Science-Based Stockpile Stewardship program to insure a high level of confidence in the safety and reliability of the stockpile. To this end, the Department of Energy Stockpile Stewardship and Management Plan (SSMP) is a comprehensive program designed to meet that requirement. The Department of Defense has worked closely with DOE in developing this plan. DOE Assistant Secretary Reis will discuss the program in more detail.

Under the SSMP, we must maintain the capability to certify weapon types in the enduring stockpile. This means we may have to modify nuclear weapons and their delivery systems in the future as parts reach the end of their design life, wear out, and are no longer in production. These modifications are not prohibited by the CTBT, only nuclear weapon test explosions are prohibited. We will require that the stockpile continue to remain safe, secure and reliable into the future.

While there is no current need to produce new nuclear warhead designs, Administration policy requires that DOE maintain the capability to respond to potential future requirements. DOE must demonstrate the capability to refabricate and certify weapons types in the enduring stockpile. It must also maintain the capability to design, fabricate and certify new nuclear warheads.

A critical element of stewardship is tritium. If "new" tritium is not available sometime near the middle of the next decade, the U.S. could be forced to make unilateral reductions in deployed forces, or to otherwise modify our deterrent posture for lack of technical and material support. We anticipate and eagerly await a decision from DOE in the very near future on its preferred approach to producing tritium that will meet our future stockpile requirements.

Under Safeguard F, associated with the CTBT, President Clinton directed the Secretaries of Defense and Energy to certify to the President whether the Nation's nuclear stockpile remains safe and reliable without the need for nuclear explosive tests. The certification is based on an assessment by the Nation's chief nuclear managers, operators, and scientists (i.e., the joint Nuclear Weapons Council, the Commander-in-Chief of the Strategic Command, and the Directors of the nuclear weapons laboratories). If our experts advised us they could no longer certify the safety and reliability of a weapon type critical to our national deterrent without testing, the Secretaries would inform the President, who would be prepared, in consultation with Congress, to withdraw from the Treaty under the supreme national interest clause and conduct appropriate nuclear tests required to fix the problem. We consider this possibility to be remote given a properly supported and executed stockpile stewardship and management program.

Another CTBT matter of extreme importance is the verifiability of the Treaty. We believe the Treaty is verifiable but recognize that the monitoring challenges presented by its wide scope exceed those imposed by any previous nuclear test-related treaty. One of the President's conditions for the Treaty is to continue a comprehensive research and development program to improve our treaty monitoring capabilities and operations. Therefore, our current capability to monitor nuclear explosions will undergo significant improvement over the next several years to meet the monitoring challenges.

There are, of course, conceivable CTBT evasion scenarios. However, the Administration believes the Treaty is effectively verifiable because the U.S. has a wide range of resources (e.g., National Intelligence Means, the totality of information available in public and private channels, and the mechanisms established by the Treaty) for addressing compliance concerns and imposing sanctions in cases of noncompliance. Thus, we will have the means to assess whether the Treaty is deterring the conduct of a series of nuclear explosions that, in terms of the numbers and yields of tests, could undermine U.S. security interests. These verification means would enable us to take prompt and effective counteraction.

For the authoritative estimate of U.S. monitoring capabilities with respect to the CTBT, I refer you to the recently completed National Intelligence Estimate, "Monitoring the Comprehensive Test Ban Treaty Over The Next 10 Years."

Thus, the Administration's judgment that the CTBT is effectively verifiable also reflects the belief that U.S. nuclear deterrence would not be undermined by the numbers and yields of possible nuclear tests that the United States might fail to detect under the Treaty.

Mr. Chairman, this concludes my prepared statement. I will be happy to take your questions now or for the record.

STATEMENT OF HAROLD P. SMITH, JR., ASSISTANT TO THE SECRETARY OF DEFENSE FOR ATOMIC ENERGY (NUCLEAR AND CHEMICAL AND BIOLOGICAL DEFENSE PROGRAMS)

Senator DOMENICI. Thank you very much.

Now, I would like Dr. Smith to explain how the DOD develops specific criteria. How do we decide which warheads with which capabilities are necessary?

I want him to explain what the President meant when he said we will maintain our nuclear deterrent. Does that mean we can do without some designs if problems come up? If so, which ones do we need and which ones do we not need? Or do we have a management structure that can make that kind of decision?

Dr. Smith.

Dr. SMITH. Thank you, Mr. Chairman, Senator Cochran, Senator Reid. For the record, Mr. Chairman, I would like to note that the Junior in my name goes with Smith, not with the Junior Assistant to the Secretary. With a name like "Smith, one needs all of the identification that one can obtain. [Laughter.]

Dr. SMITH. Mr. Chairman, I would like to submit my written testimony for the record and address the questions that you just directed to me.

Senator DOMENICI. It will be accepted.

Dr. SMITH. Thank you, sir.

When Dr. Reis and I took office in 1993, we did not know it but we strongly suspected that the United States had just conducted its last nuclear test. Starting with that point, Dr. Reis and I have jointly and collegially, built the program that currently is before you now.

We started with concepts: That is, we knew that there were problems associated with not testing, and we knew that there were solutions, whether they be fast computers or particularly new facilities. We had to develop a plan to apply those solutions to the various problems. And, of course, we are now to the point where we have actually developed a program—that is, resources are being placed against those plans to solve the problems that come up.

You might say in the beginning, in 1993, Dr. Reis and I had to guess what this program would cost. Later on, we had to estimate what it would cost. And now I think we are to the point where we can calculate what it will cost.

All of this is captured in the vehicle called the Green Book, which is, in fact, a clear, detailed program plan developing by DOE under the auspices of the Nuclear Weapons Council. I think we did remarkably well. The initial guesses were about $4 billion per year. The current budget, which Secretary Peña mentioned, is about $4.5 billion a year. To have been within 12 percent in this brave new world of no nuclear testing I think is quite a remarkable accomplishment. I give my colleague, Dr. Reis, the greater part of the credit for developing that program.

Now our job is to program scarce and competing resources against the very demanding requirements of a world with nuclear arsenals but no nuclear tests. The funds for the DOE and DOD nuclear weapons activities are derived from a large, common defense account, fondly known as 050.

In 1988, fortunately, Congress created the Nuclear Weapons Council and authorized that it develop nuclear weapons stockpile options, evaluate the costs of those options, and coordinate budget matters between the two Departments.

I think the Congress is to be congratulated. The NWC, the Nuclear Weapons Council, is ideally constituted to apply these resources to the tasks in a prioritized manner.

It is my pleasure to chair the standing committee that supports the Nuclear Weapons Council. It has been meeting monthly for many, many months. We recently decided that it was essential that we reexamine from stem to stern the nuclear requirements, eventually leading to the DOE program.

Mr. Miller, my colleague, only last month reviewed carefully the policy by which we set these requirements. In the ensuing months, the Joint Chiefs of Staff will convert that policy once again to requirements, and General Habiger, as Commander of STRATCOM, will convert those to actual war plans, eventually leading, of course, to the DOE program that Dr. Reis could discuss in detail.

We must insure that adequate funds are provided to both Departments to have a safe, reliable, and effective nuclear deterrent. Further, these costs must be balanced against a wide assortment of national defense priorities. The Nuclear Weapons Council will work through the established, deliberative procedures to insure that the nuclear programs compete effectively against other important and high priority programs for funding adequate to meet the broad requirements of national security.

Senator Reid, the chairman had asked if I could address the manner by which we come to the requirements. I have given you the procedures and in closed session, I will be happy to go into more detail.

I can say in this session that for each arm of the TRIAD, there are two separate warheads, so that we can face systemic failure of one type of warhead on each leg of the TRIAD and yet still maintain that TRIAD. I will go into greater detail, if you would like, in the closed session.

If I may, I would like to also discuss——

Senator COCHRAN [presiding]. I am serving as the chairman in the absence of Senator Domenici, our chairman.

Dr. SMITH. You can always tell a Democrat. Thank you, Senator.

Mr. Cochran, would you like me to discuss——

Senator COCHRAN. I would like for you to answer the questions that Senator Domenici outlined that he would like to have answered.

Senator REID. We are going to have a closed session, Thad, a little bit later. He said that some of them he cannot answer here.

Senator COCHRAN. Yes, I heard that.

VERIFICATION OF TREATY VIOLATIONS

Dr. SMITH. I would like then briefly to go to the verification of the CTBT, another important question before this committee.

First of all, there is nothing theoretical about our capability to verify nuclear explosions. We, the United States, have applied many resources for many years to just this problem. It is not perfect. There are some low yields which we would not detect. I will leave to my colleague, Dr. Reis, if you so desire, to discuss what the impact would be of not detecting such low-yield devices.

But we do have a high level of confidence that we will detect rather modest nuclear explosions and, more than that, anyone who should choose to have a nuclear explosion, to conduct a nuclear test, would have to live in a world in which the CTB and the signatories of the CTB would be well aware that such a test had been conducted.

In short, there is a form of deterrence here.

There are four different approaches to verifying nuclear explosions. First, there is our own intelligence capability. Second, the treaty itself allows for onsite inspections, which is a new arm of how we verify whether or not a nuclear explosion has taken place. Third, there are bilateral agreements, including Russia, France,

United Kingdom, and we think next month we will have a similar agreement with the Kazakhs. Finally, there are open sources, and these are not to be taken lightly. Universities, laboratories, oil exploration all have the kinds of instrumentation which can detect in one form or another nuclear explosions.

The technologies involved here are legion. We have netted seismic arrays. We have seismic stations. We have an array of detectors. We have low frequency sound detection. We have hydroacoustics. And, although not part of the treaty, our own intelligence community provides sensors that include optical, gamma ray, x ray, neutron, electromagnetic pulse. These are part of our national technical means. They are not part of the CTB. But they are all overlapping and they are all complementary.

So the challenge is can we maintain an arsenal without testing and can we verify compliance if there should be a test. In my opinion, we should accept that challenge. The odds are favorable and the benefits are legion.

Thank you very much, Mr. Chairman. I await your further questions.

[The statement follows:]

PREPARED STATEMENT OF HAROLD P. SMITH, JR.

Mr. Chairman and members of the Subcommittee, I am honored to have this opportunity to appear before you today. As the principal advisor to the Secretary of Defense on matters relating to the nuclear weapons stockpile my remarks today will focus on the Stockpile Stewardship and Management Program (SSMP), the role of the Nuclear Weapons Council for which I am the Executive Secretary and how the Departments of Defense and Energy may continue to ensure high confidence in our Nation's nuclear weapons stockpile within the constraints imposed by a Comprehensive Test Ban.

Nuclear weapons will continue to be an essential element of national security strategy, and the maintenance of a safe and reliable nuclear stockpile remains a supreme national interest of the United States. The Department of Energy's Stockpile Stewardship and Management Program was created to provide the tools, infrastructure, and personnel necessary to ensure a high level of confidence in the stockpile.

In the past, nuclear testing was the sine qua non for confidence in the Nation's stockpile. The challenge facing the Departments of Defense and Energy is to maintain a high level of confidence indefinitely, in a cost effective manner, without nuclear testing. The SSMP was developed with the support of the Secretary of Defense and the Chairman of the Joint Chiefs of Staff to meet this challenge. It is no coincidence that these three organizations (DOE, DOD, and JCS) also provide the principal representatives to the joint organization responsible for the task of developing nuclear weapons stockpile options and the costs of such options the congressionally established Nuclear Weapons Council (NWC).

More than any other deliberative group, the NWC is the most authoritative body concerned with the overall management of the nuclear stockpile. As an interdepartmental organization, the NWC is supported by a wide range of disciplines: security and safety experts, policy makers, managers, maintainers, and operators. Membership of the NWC consists of the Under Secretary of Defense (Acquisition and Technology) who chairs the Council, the Vice Chairman of the Joint Chiefs of Staff, and a representative of the Department of Energy as designated by the Secretary of Energy. Today, the DOE member is Deputy Secretary Moler. The council is supported by the flag and general officer Standing and Safety Committee, which I chair.

The activities of the NWC reflect the monumental scope of the SSMP and the efforts put forth by both Departments to implement an effective and efficient program. As you know, the enabling legislation for the Nuclear Weapons Council charges the Council with responsibility for developing costs for various stockpile options and states that the Council will be responsible for:

(1) Preparing the Nuclear Weapons Stockpile Memorandum.

(2) Developing nuclear weapons stockpile options costs.

(3) Coordinating programming and budget matters pertaining to nuclear weapons programs between the Department of Defense and the Department of Energy.

48-165 98 - 3

(4) Identifying various options for cost-effective schedules for nuclear weapons production.

(5) Considering safety, security, and control issues for existing weapons and for proposed new weapon program starts.

(6) Ensuring that adequate consideration is given to design, performance, and cost tradeoffs for all proposed new nuclear weapon programs.

(7) Providing broad guidance regarding priorities for research on nuclear weapons.

(8) Coordinating and approving activities conducted by the Department of Energy for the study, development, production, and retirement of nuclear warheads, including concept definition studies, feasibility studies, engineering development, hardware component fabrication, warhead production, and warhead retirement.

(9) Preparing comments on annual proposals for budget levels for research on nuclear weapons and transmitting those comments to the Secretary of Defense and the Secretary of Energy before the preparation of the annual budget requests by the Secretaries of those Departments.

The Council's primary focus is to provide the guidance necessary for both Departments to maintain a safe, secure, and reliable nuclear weapons stockpile while at the same time ensure the efficient and effective operation of the supporting infrastructure. I would like to provide one example of how the process can work to the benefit of all.

The President established the current Annual Certification process in August 1995 to ascertain on a yearly basis whether the stockpile remains safe and reliable under a comprehensive test ban. Since then, the Departments of Defense and Energy, the Commander of Strategic Command, the Directors of the National Laboratories, the Services, and Joint Staff have worked diligently to implement a timely and meaningful process. The Chairman of the Joint Chiefs of Staff specifically required that the process be both credible and enduring.

Over the course of the last two years, those most involved in implementing the new Annual Certification process have developed a well thought out approach. In 1996, the NWC completed its first report to the President on stockpile certification. The second annual report has been approved by the Secretary of Defense, and will be signed by both Secretaries for transmission to the President soon. As a result of the close cooperation, I am confident that the current process meets the requirements stated by both the Chairman and the President and that they will be able to certify again this year, as last, that there is no need to return to underground nuclear testing.

The NWC and the NWC Standing and Safety Committee have striven diligently as both Departments and the Services adjusted their strategies, requirements, and capabilities to fit a post Cold War world. Some of the highlights include:

—September 1991: Production of several planned new weapons halted by Presidential initiative.
—September 1992: Last underground test.
—July 1993: Test moratorium extended.
—October 1993: Interagency Task Force Report, "Plan for Stockpile Stewardship Under a Test Ban".
—November 1993: Stockpile Stewardship established.
—May 1995: First Stockpile Stewardship and Management Program Plan.
—February 1996 fiscal year 1996 SSMP Released First "Green Book" and Initial matching of costs to tasks.
—October 1997: Fiscal year 1997 SSMP Draft Second Green Book.

Allow me to now present two brief success stories from the past year which illustrate the kind of effectiveness that exemplifies the NWC process.

The first involves the retirement of the B53 bomb. Mr. Chairman, I told you of this program when I testified before your Subcommittee earlier this year so I will only briefly touch upon it here. Because it was designed almost 40 years ago, the B53 did not meet modern nuclear safety standards. The system that replaced it, the B61–11, is a modern system that meets current standards for safety, security, and use control. Due in large part to active participation from the organizations represented by the NWC, the replacement program was implemented in a remarkably short time only 16 months from initial verbal authorization to delivery of the first retrofit kits. The drive to replace the B53 made a significant contribution to the safety and effectiveness of the enduring stockpile and is an outstanding example of enlightened stockpile management.

I particularly want to emphasize that the B61–11 is a non-nuclear modification of the previously fielded B61–7. The two weapons contain the same physics package, so there are no requirements for nuclear testing.

Secondly, the NWC coordinated the initiative for resuming subcritical experiments at the Nevada Test Site earlier this year. These experiments are necessary to study the performance of nuclear materials in an aging stockpile. They do not involve a nuclear yield or a nuclear explosion. Hence, they are not prohibited by a Comprehensive Test Ban. The NWC reviewed the technical merit of these experiments and recommended they proceed. The data derived from these experiments are essential if we are to maintain our nuclear deterrent into the future without the benefit of nuclear testing. Experiments such as these are crucial to retaining a cadre of weapons scientists at the national laboratories and an important aspect of a dynamic program of stockpile stewardship.

Initiatives such as these illustrate the fact that the nuclear weapons program has evolved significantly since the end of the Cold War. The relationship between the Department of Defense and the Department of Energy, which I have described as one of customer and supplier, continues to evolve in response to these monumental changes. The good news is that despite the changes, the Council remains a dynamic, authoritative and deliberative body.

Mr. Chairman, in your letter of invitation, you asked us to address nuclear weapons requirements and how these requirements are set. Let me say briefly that requirements stem from our national policy. The broad outlines of that policy have been in place for years, but in 1994, President Clinton's Nuclear Posture Review recognized that while the strategic environment had been transformed, nuclear weapons would continue to play a critical role in deterring aggression against the U.S., its overseas forces, and our allies and friends.

Having reaffirmed our policy of a continued nuclear deterrent, the Office of the Secretary of Defense and the Joint Staff develop the strategy needed to support that policy. The military Commanders in Chief, including General Habiger, Commander of Strategic Command, develop the employment plans to support that strategy. Nuclear weapons numbers and types evolve from those plans. The President then completes the process by approving these weapon numbers and types in the annual Nuclear Weapons Stockpile Memorandum.

General Habiger and I have spoken on many occasions about the adequacy of our current stockpile and I will leave it to him to comment in more detail. While we must maintain the capability to certify weapon types in the enduring stockpile, for my part, I see no current need to produce new-design nuclear weapons. Of course we will have to modify nuclear weapons and their delivery systems in the future as parts reach the end of their design life, wear out, and are no longer in production. These modifications do not involve the nuclear warhead and are not affected by the proposed CTBT.

I would now like to address the other issue which has been raised by this committee, that is, our ability to verify test ban treaty compliance by others.

I would like to state at the outset that a technical monitoring system will always operate down to some limit greater than zero-yield. The U.S. has sought a practical, proven, cost-effective approach which will provide an acceptable level of confidence, a deterrent to violations and an interlocking web of constraints that promotes effective verification.

The challenges of monitoring a global ban on nuclear testing exceed those imposed by any previous nuclear-test related treaty. The United States has a long history in the practical application of monitoring technologies. To meet the new challenges, the United States will use a wide assortment of resources that include our national intelligence means, all the information available to the intelligence community, from both technical and non-technical sources and from public and private channels.

Since the detection of the Soviet Union's first nuclear test in 1949, the United States has maintained and has continued to develop a robust monitoring network of sensors and analytical techniques. Today, the United States maintains seismic and hydroacoustic sensors for the detection of explosions underground and in the ocean, air sampling sensors for detection of nuclear explosions in the atmosphere and detection of effluents from underground nuclear testing, and sensors onboard satellites for explosions in the atmosphere and space.

The verification regime called for in the Treaty includes an International Monitoring System (IMS), composed of global networks of seismic, hydroacoustic, infrasound and radionuclide sensors, a global communications network infrastructure to collect the data from these systems and an International Data Center (IDC) to receive and process these data and provide both data and analysis results to all Parties of the Treaty.

The quality of these international networks are expected to meet U.S. national standards. This system is designed to provide high quality detection of signals from an underground, underwater or atmospheric nuclear explosion to a level well below one kiloton when no evasive action is taken. For example, the seismic and hydroacoustic networks are expected to detect non-evasive tests of less than one kiloton in the northern hemisphere.

Although each of the international sensor networks has been designed to be operated independently, the combined capability of the IMS is enhanced by the complementarity of the several international sensor networks. When one sensor network detects a signal, other networks look for corroborating patterns. The international system and the U.S. national systems are also complementary. For example, the established U.S. national systems tend to be focused on monitoring areas which have in the past been of greatest concern to the United States, while the international systems provide a more balanced global coverage.

The result is a layered, synergistic approach to U.S. monitoring where treaty and national mechanisms combine to improve our overall capability for monitoring nuclear testing worldwide.

The International Monitoring System is being implemented by a Preparatory Commission which began work earlier this year in Vienna, Austria. The U.S. is working with the Commission to establish a rigorous environment in which this equipment would operate. A number of sites which were originally established as part of the United States monitoring system will be incorporated into the new international system. The most complete international system is the seismic network, with 34 of the 50 primary detection stations already in place and transmitting data to the prototype International Data Center.

The Department of Defense has in place an agreement with the Russian Federation to cooperate with the development and installation of IMS seismic array facilities in that country and agreements with several other countries are pending. Current plans call for the IMS networks to be operational within about three years.

At the center of the international verification regime is the technically advanced International Data Center (IDC). This center must detect and locate tens of thousands of events on an annual basis with an unprecedented level of sensitivity and accuracy. The United States has taken a leading role in the development of the International Data Center and the prototype is currently operating in Arlington, Virginia. The United States will work with the Preparatory Commission to transition this facility to Vienna, Austria over the next three years. The same data processing technology is also being incorporated into the U.S. systems to handle and analyze data from our national systems.

Both the Department of Defense and the Department of Energy have development programs to provide the required technical support to the monitoring and compliance systems which will be used by the United States. Both Departments will respond positively to the treaty Safeguard requiring a continuation of the comprehensive research and development program to improve out treaty monitoring capabilities and operations. In this regard, I would like to acknowledge the unique contribution that the Department of Energy's national laboratories have made to U.S. verification capabilities, especially in the fields of seismic sensors and on-site inspection technologies.

There are, however, evasion measures a potential violator could employ to evade detection of a nuclear explosion or to obscure his identity as the party responsible for the explosion. Because of this, the U.S. will have difficulty monitoring very low-yield tests in all environments with high confidence. Such evasive measures have been and will continue to be carefully studied. It should be noted that the CTBT establishes some mechanisms to provide information about ambiguous events that we would not have otherwise. Moreover, if a significant gap or weaknesses in the overall compliance regime is identified in the future, further improvements in sensor capabilities would be programmed and implemented.

In closing, our current capability to monitor nuclear explosions will undergo significant improvements over the next several years to meet the challenges of a global nuclear test ban. The United States will have at its disposal a wide range of resources, including those of our national systems, and those from the treaty monitoring mechanisms, for addressing compliance concerns. The United States will therefore have the means to assess whether U.S. national security interests are being damaged by potential compliance concerns.

It is therefore our judgment that a global nuclear test ban is effectively verifiable with the means provided by our intelligence capabilities, together with the Treaty's verification regime, and our diplomatic efforts.

In conclusion, the loss of testing changes the way the national laboratories, the Department of Energy, and the Department of Defense will establish confidence. We are in the process of transitioning from an empirical system based on nuclear tests to a science based program that will enhance our understanding of nuclear weapons processes, and our ability to model them. In the United States, we have been preparing for this transition for over five years. We are the vanguard of the world's effort to reduce the threat of nuclear proliferation while we ensure our Nation's security.

The Department of Energy has a comprehensive program designed to ensure that our weapons remain safe and reliable in the absence of nuclear testing. The Department of Defense endorses this program. For its part, the Department of Defense will be actively involved in defining SSMP program elements and priorities. We look forward to working closely with the Department of Energy to effectively manage program responsibilities in the years to come.

We also strongly support the principle that if the SSMP does not meet its objectives and the DOD and DOE cannot certify the reliability of a critical element of our deterrent without nuclear testing, the United States would give the most serious consideration to exercising its right under the Test Ban Treaty to withdraw from the treaty under the "supreme national interest" clause (Safeguard F) for the purpose of conducting such necessary tests. The President regards that possibility as remote, given a properly supported and executed stewardship program. But to be successful, we need the support of not only the Administration, but also bipartisan support from the Congress.

In short, today and for the future, assuming the SSMP program is adequately funded and successfully executed, my confidence in the safety and reliability of our nuclear deterrent force will remain strong. The Stockpile Stewardship and Management program is designed to provide the tools to maintain this confidence well into the future.

DEPARTMENT OF ENERGY

STATEMENT OF DR. VICTOR H. REIS, ASSISTANT SECRETARY OF ENERGY FOR DEFENSE PROGRAMS

Senator DOMENICI [presiding]. Thank you.

Dr. Reis, before you start, I want to pay tribute to you. I think, while there have been many collaborators, obviously without your vision we would not be where we are on the science-based stockpile stewardship. And while it still has a way to go before it is implemented, obviously, and a way to go before we know how effective it is or will have been, I very much think what you have done is something very significant for the Nation and I want to congratulate you on that.

Senator REID. Senator Domenici, that was very nice of you to do that. I think that is very like you. Not only is it important what he has done for our country, but for the world.

Senator DOMENICI. Thank you very much.

Dr. Reis, would you proceed.

Dr. REIS. Thank you, Senator Domenici, and thank you as well, Senator Reid, for your kind comments. Again, thank you also for the opportunity to testify before you today on the Stockpile Stewardship Program. This is a program that is fundamental to our national security under a comprehensive test ban. I would like to begin with a brief history of stockpile stewardship, tell you what it is, give you its current status, and then, of course, when we are in closed session, we will answer any of your questions.

In addition to my written testimony, I would like to provide the subcommittee with a recently published overview on the program and, if you wish, submit it for the record. I think you have copies of that.

Senator DOMENICI. Thank you.

[The information follows:]

STOCKPILE STEWARDSHIP PROGRAM

OVERVIEW AND PROGRESS

PREFACE

In the early 1990's, as part of its continuing world leadership role in the arms control arena, the U.S. halted production of new nuclear warheads and conducted its last nuclear explosive test. Thus ended an era in which the U.S. modernized its nuclear weapons stockpile by continually replacing aging systems with new systems and in which nuclear testing served as the ultimate arbiter of the safety, reliability, and performance of the nation's nuclear weapons stockpile.

With the decision to cease production of new nuclear warheads and end nuclear testing, the nation now faces the challenge of maintaining its existing nuclear weapons stockpile with other tools and different kinds of tests. To meet this challenge, the Department of Energy has developed a Stockpile Stewardship Program. The strategy and key components of this new approach are described in the May 1995 DOE report "The Stockpile Stewardship and Management Program: Maintaining Confidence in the Safety and Reliability of the Enduring U.S. Nuclear Weapon

Stockpile." This overview and progress report updates the 1995 report and describes the program accomplishments to date.

Since the genesis of the Stockpile Stewardship Program in 1992, significant progress has been made. A Record of Decision on the Programmatic Environmental Impact Statement was issued in December 1996, establishing the architecture for the future U.S. weapons complex. An implementation plan for the Stockpile Stewardship Program (the Green Book) has been developed and is already in its second annual revision. The Presidentially mandated first Annual Certification of the stockpile was completed in February 1997, and many new capabilities and facilities for the Stockpile Stewardship Program are well under way. The Dual-Axis Radiographic Hydrodynamic Test Facility is under construction, and the groundbreaking ceremony for the National Ignition Facility has taken place. Industry has begun delivering the advanced computers required for the Accelerated Strategic Computing Initiative, and record-breaking teraops (one trillion operations per second) operation has already been demonstrated. The first and second subcritical experiments, "Rebound" and "Holog," were successfully completed at the Nevada Test Site on July 2 and September 18, 1997, respectively. A life extension process for the enduring stockpile is being developed, and the dismantlement of U.S. nuclear warheads retired from the stockpile is continuing. The assets of the Stockpile Stewardship Program were applied to a modification of the B61 bomb, and we are on track to restore the nation's capability to produce tritium.

As experience is gained in assessing the safety and reliability of the enduring U.S. nuclear stockpile without nuclear testing, key program strategies of the Stockpile Stewardship Program have evolved and become better focused. In this report, an overview of the current program is presented along with the highlights of the Department of Energy's accomplishments and progress to date.

Maintaining the U.S. nuclear weapons stockpile in this new era will continue to challenge our best capabilities. The Stockpile Stewardship Program must be implemented promptly and fully. In particular, new facilities and capabilities must be developed and validated while personnel with nuclear-test experience are still available. In addition, we will continue to rely on peer review between the three weapons laboratories as a key element of the Stockpile Stewardship Program. Despite the wide-ranging challenges and risks, we are confident that this program provides the framework and capabilities for success.

VICTOR H. REIS,
Assistant Secretary for Defense Programs, U.S. Department of Energy.

PREPARED STATEMENT FROM PRESIDENT CLINTON

SUPREME NATIONAL INTEREST

As part of our national security strategy, the United States must and will retain strategic nuclear forces sufficient to deter any future hostile foreign leadership with access to strategic nuclear forces. In this regard, I consider the maintenance of a safe and reliable nuclear stockpile to be a supreme national interest of the United States.

I am assured by the Secretary of Energy and the Directors of our nuclear weapons labs that we can meet the challenge of maintaining our nuclear deterrent under a Comprehensive Test Ban Treaty through a science-based stockpile stewardship program without nuclear testing.

PRESIDENT CLINTON,
August 11, 1995.

ADDRESSING STOCKPILE STEWARDSHIP PROGRAM CHALLENGES

Over the past five years, the Department of Energy's Stockpile Stewardship Program has evolved from a vision for the future to an implemented plan of action. While the program's fundamental objective is unchanged from previous years—that is, to maintain high confidence in the safety, reliability, and performance of the U.S. nuclear weapons stockpile—the conditions under which this objective must be accomplished have changed greatly since the early 1990's. The Department of Energy (DOE) is meeting and will continue to meet an unprecedented challenge—namely, to maintain high confidence in the safety, reliability, and performance of the nation's nuclear weapon stockpile by using nonnuclear experiments and computer simulations in lieu of underground nuclear testing.

—*No nuclear testing.*—The Comprehensive Test Ban Treaty (CTBT), which was signed by the President in September 1996 and submitted to the Senate for ratification on September 23, 1997, prohibits nuclear testing unless the involved State Party invokes the "supreme national interest" clause and withdraws from the treaty. Currently, there is high confidence in the safety, reliability, and performance of the nuclear warheads in the enduring stockpile. This confidence is based on understanding gained from 50 years experience and more than 1,000 nuclear tests, including the results of approximately 150 nuclear tests of modern weapon types during the last 20 years. The President has expressed his confidence in the ability of the Department of Energy to maintain the U.S. nuclear deterrent without nuclear testing. In response, the DOE's nuclear weapons stewards have directed their combined energies to developing new nonnuclear experimental facilities (National Ignition Facility [NIF], Dual-Axis Radiographic Hydrodynamic Test Facility [DARHT]), a world-class computational capability to enable simulation of complex nuclear explosions, and the conduct of subcritical experiments at the Nevada Test Site.

—*Tritium production.*—The United States has not produced tritium for nuclear warheads since 1988 and will require a new tritium production source possibly as early as 2005. A dual-track approach using a commercial light water reactor and accelerator production of tritium is being vigorously pursued.

—*An aging stockpile.*—Nuclear warheads are not static objects. Materials change over time (e.g., radioactive decay, embrittlement, corrosion). Some of these changes do not adversely affect warhead safety, reliability, or performance; but others may, and some are yet unknown. With the average age of the stockpile now being 14 years—older than ever before—it is expected that new problems will arise. In addition, a number of warheads are approaching the end of their originally anticipated deployment period. To meet this challenge, each of the stockpiled warheads is undergoing a thorough assessment to determine vulnerabilities and to establish refurbishment schedules that will ensure stockpile life extension.

—*An aging cadre of stockpile stewards.*—Many of the scientists and engineers with actual weapons design, production, and test experience have already retired, and most of those remaining are within ten years of retirement. A new generation of weapons scientists and engineers must be trained and their competence validated before the current generation leaves the workforce. Knowledge preservation programs are underway that include video-recording the experiences of senior designers as well as the mentoring of new stockpile stewards. The senior designers are also reviewing archived nuclear weapon test data and showing the future stewards how to interpret and extract useful information previously not needed when nuclear tests were conducted.

—*A smaller less diverse stockpile.*—The nation's stockpile now has fewer warheads and fewer warhead types than at any time since the 1960's. Thus, the U.S. nuclear deterrent is more susceptible to common process and common component failures. A new annual certification process and an enhanced surveillance process have been initiated to ensure that potential problems are found before the safety and reliability of the stockpile is degraded.

—*No requirements for new-design nuclear warhead production.*—Without new production programs, warheads will remain in the stockpile well beyond their anticipated lifetimes and beyond the Department of Energy's base of experience. Without requirements for new warheads, existing warheads will be refurbished and modified to extend their lifetimes. To address this challenge, the capability is being maintained to design and fabricate replacement warhead parts, as well as to design replacement warheads for existing stockpiled weapons.

—*A reconfigured production complex.*—The production complex of the Cold War years is being downsized and consolidated. The future capability-based complex, with its reduced capacity, will not be configured for high-rate production programs. Thus, improved manufacturing processes, including the integration of system design, component design, and process development, will be needed to achieve timely production at a reduced cost. To address this challenge, a Programmatic Environmental Impact Statement was developed that specifies significant reductions in the size of the DOE nuclear weapons complex and the development of an agile, capability-based manufacturing enterprise that will use advanced design and production techniques to respond to both normal and contingency requirements.

The focus of the Stockpile Stewardship Program (SSP) is the U.S. nuclear stockpile. All elements of the program are directed at ensuring the safety, reliability, and performance of this stockpile. As stated in the above responses to each program challenge and as described in more detail throughout this document, we will develop the fundamental understanding needed to ensure the ability to anticipate and fix problems and to deal with future unknowns before they affect stockpile safety or reliability.

At the heart of the Stockpile Stewardship Program is the issue of confidence. Confidence in the weapons is achieved through the effective management of the system that maintains the weapons and the expert judgment of the people who assess them. The ultimate measure of success for the Stockpile Stewardship Program is to certify that the stockpile remains safe and reliable without a recommendation to the President that nuclear testing is required.

The first annual certification of the nuclear weapons stockpile has been completed, and both the Department of Defense (DOD) and DOE have concluded that the stockpile is safe and reliable and that there is no need to conduct a nuclear test. The second annual certification process is currently underway and is on schedule.

STOCKPILE STEWARDSHIP PROGRAM INTEGRATION

A distinguishing feature of the Stockpile Stewardship Program is its integration. As depicted below, the Stockpile Stewardship Program (SSP) has three major elements: Surveillance, Manufacturing and Operations; Scientific and Experimental Integration; and, Strategic Computing and Simulation.

Stockpile Surveillance, Manufacturing and Operations focuses on activities that extend the life of the current stockpile, including surveillance, maintenance, refurbishment, assessment, and annual certification of the warheads. The Scientific and Experimental Integration effort involves developing advanced theoretical, computational, and experimental methods that will enable the continuing assessment and certification of warheads in the enduring stockpile without nuclear testing. The Strategic Computing and Simulation effort supports both Surveillance, Manufacturing and Operations and Scientific and Experimental Integration and includes computation, experimentation, and modeling as well as archiving and analysis of past nuclear test data.

All of the Stockpile Stewardship Program elements are seamless and continual, with no clear ending of one phase before the beginning of another. Assessment and certification pervade all activities, from surveillance through manufacturing. Likewise, computational modeling and prediction are integral to every activity, from the assessments of aging-related changes, to the design and certification of replacement components, to projections of stockpile life extension.

Not only are the laboratories and plants working closely together, particularly for surveillance and manufacturing, but the activities under each program are tightly interconnected. High-performance networks linking the advanced computers, coupled with other tools, are essential elements of this effective integration. In addition, the Department of Energy's laboratories and plants work closely with the Department of Defense to make sure that the enduring U.S. nuclear stockpile meets national security requirements.

STOCKPILE STEWARDSHIP PROGRAM STRATEGIES

The goals of the Stockpile Stewardship Program (SSP) will be achieved through an integrated surveillance, assessment, certification, design, and manufacturing process. These activities have remained constant; however, the integrating strategies have evolved as the program has matured. For example, the Stockpile Life Extension Process (SLEP) has been developed as a formal integrated activity through which the Department of Energy, laboratories, plants, and military services evaluate, plan, and schedule the specific refurbishment actions to be conducted on each weapon system. The accelerated and greatly expanded use of strategic computing and simulation tools is the fundamental innovation of this evolution. Today, the program is characterized by three integrated strategies or phases of stockpile stewardship.

—*Surveillance: predicting and detecting problems.*—Defects and aging-related changes must be identified before they can degrade warhead safety, reliability, or performance. To the extent possible, we must predict—relying on experiments coupled with computer modeling and simulation—the occurrence and impact of changes, both those that have been dealt with previously in stockpile warheads and changes that have not been encountered.

—*Assessment and Certification: analyzing and evaluating effects of changes on warhead safety and performance.*—The effects of identified and predicted age- and environment-related changes in stockpile warheads must be assessed, utilizing in large measure advanced numerical simulations and models to determine whether the changes adversely affect safety, reliability, or performance. Determinations as to whether the degradation is severe enough to require the replacement or rebuilding of warhead components or even entire weapons must be made. Evaluation and certification of new materials, new fabrication techniques, and new manufacturing processes are essential to make sure they are functionally equivalent to the originals.

—*Design and Manufacturing: refurbishing stockpile warheads and certifying new parts, materials, and processes.*—Periodically replacements must be made for limited-lifetime components (e.g., tritium reservoirs, neutron generators), and other warhead parts must be rebuilt or manufactured to replace those that have experienced or are predicted to experience detrimental aging-related changes. The new components must be certified so that defects that degrade warhead safety, performance, or reliability are not introduced into the stockpile. Advanced simulation and modeling and extensive use of archived data are critical to maintaining confidence in the rebuilt or remanufactured parts.

Predicting and Detecting Problems: Surveillance

Stockpile surveillance has been a major component of the U.S. nuclear weapons program ever since the first weapons were put into the stockpile. Approximately 14,000 weapons have been examined and subjected to a variety of nonnuclear laboratory experiments and flight tests since 1958. In cases where these nonnuclear tests could not provide conclusive answers, nuclear tests of stockpile warheads or warhead components were conducted.

Problems requiring corrective action have arisen in nuclear and nonnuclear warhead components. All of the warhead types in the enduring U.S. stockpile have had repairs or retrofits, and several have required repairs to the nuclear package.

Without the replacement of older warheads with new warheads, the stockpile will age beyond the experience base. The Department of Energy has never before had large numbers of 30-, 40-, or 50-year-old warheads in the stockpile. (The average age of a stockpile warhead has always been less than 13 years.) As a result, new types of aging-related changes and problems in these older warheads are expected to be encountered.

To succeed in this new reality, new surveillance methods and predictive capabilities are needed so that the full range of problems that may arise in the enduring stockpile can be detected. There is also a need to predict and identify aging-related changes and to understand the significance of these changes and their effect on warhead safety and performance. Some changes have little or no effect, whereas others can make a major difference.

Defects occur throughout the lifetime of a warhead. Typically in complex manufactured systems, initial defects associated with design or fabrication form a large fraction of all defects found. With a high sampling rate during the early years, these defects can be detected and corrected. During middle age, the defect rate typically declines to a lower but nonzero level. As a system ages and components deteriorate, the defect rate climbs. The U.S. nuclear stockpile has followed the pattern of these first two stages. We have limited experience with the third stage and must develop the capability to predict when it will be reached.

The goal of enhanced surveillance is to predict or detect the precursors and onset of aging-related defects before they jeopardize warhead safety, reliability, or performance. Predictive modeling and simulation are central to this activity. With sufficient lead time, the necessary redesigns, refurbishments, and recertifications can be made efficiently and cost effectively within the capabilities and capacity of the downsized production complex.

An enhanced surveillance process has been established to develop the technologies and methods as well as the fundamental understanding of materials properties and weapons science to significantly improve detection and predictive capabilities. The major activities to be pursued are:

—Testing and researching the aging-related behavior of existing stockpile materials, components, and systems, including those from retired warheads.

—Developing improved computational models of materials aging and materials performance.

—Developing and conducting high-fidelity (i.e., enhanced data acquisition) nonnuclear flight tests to examine the behavior of nearly all actual warhead components in realistic environments. (Historically, most flight tests, for example, did not include realistic simulation of the nuclear package.)

—Developing techniques for advanced analysis of existing surveillance data, including complex numerical models and simulations as well as improved access to and analysis of archived data.

As these enhanced surveillance technologies and methods are prototyped and validated, they will be integrated into the core stockpile surveillance process. Improved predictions of component lifetimes, made possible through enhanced surveillance, are key to the strategy for extending indefinitely the life of stockpile warheads.

Analyzing and Evaluating: Assessment and Certification

Data and test results must be analyzed, assessed, and evaluated before conclusions can be drawn as to the safety, reliability, or performance of stockpile warheads. The Assessment and Certification Processes are designed to:

—Develop an ability to predict and understand the lifetime and aging-related changes that occur in every warhead component.

—Identify and understand significant changes, variables, and processes in terms of warhead safety, reliability, and performance.

—Validate new experimental and computational tools.

—Validate new manufacturing processes and materials to ensure that rebuilt components and warheads are equivalent to the originals.

—Develop and demonstrate the judgment of the next generation of weapons scientists and engineers.

The science and engineering of nuclear explosives are extremely complex. There are many parameters and unknowns that greatly influence the performance of nuclear warheads. Some of these have, in the past, been identified only in nuclear test failures. Even when nuclear testing was permitted, the weapons scientists and engineers were never able to test nuclear warheads to a statistical certainty. In addition, various testing constraints (e.g., the Threshold Test Ban Treaty) required extrapolations to evaluate full-warhead performance and safety characteristics. The key to accurate extrapolations, then as now, is the expert judgment of the weapons scientists.

Now more than ever before, confidence in the accuracy of the judgment of the weapons scientists and engineers and confidence in the safety and reliability of the U.S. nuclear stockpile are closely linked. In the past, a weapon steward's judgment was developed and validated through nuclear testing and new warhead development. The Stockpile Stewardship Program is developing other means for honing and demonstrating the expert judgment of the next generation of stockpile stewards.

This is being accomplished through the integrated management of computational simulation, applied scientific research, and nonnuclear experiments. In particular, experiments are being designed that test and expand the boundaries of our understanding. There are many areas of warhead operation that cannot be adequately addressed with existing tools and the current knowledge base of the weapons scientists and engineers. To close these gaps, the Stockpile Stewardship Program is making significant investments in enhanced computational capabilities and advanced facilities for above ground experiments.

Of particular concern is the assessment challenge posed by the unrecognized problem—the "unknown unknown." The Department of Energy must have rigorous computational and experimental processes that not only confirm and extend what is known and expected but also to discover gaps in our current understanding. This ability to fill in the gaps is especially important in those areas where previously nuclear testing would have been used to bound the margins of our concerns. Therefore, an aggressive verification and validation process for both the tools and the results is needed.

The Stockpile Stewardship Program provides for demonstration-based assessment and certification of warhead safety and reliability. In the absence of nuclear testing, different experiments and tools must be relied on to obtain data relevant to nuclear warhead performance. A suite of enhanced capabilities that are needed to fill in the knowledge gaps and provide data relevant to various stockpile concerns has been identified (see chart below). Advanced experimental facilities will provide high-resolution data on the stages of the nuclear explosion—primary implosion, boost, primary-to-secondary coupling, weapon effects, etc. Wherever possible, the goal is to obtain data experimentally by more than one method.

CAPABILITIES NEEDED TO ENSURE HIGH CONFIDENCE IN WARHEAD SAFETY AND RELIABILITY

Weapon physics	Computer simulation	DARHT	Subcritical experiments	NIF	Pulsed power	LANSCE
Improved physical modes	X	X	X	X	X	X
Early implosion	X	X	X	....	....	X
Preboost	X	X	X	X	X	X
Boost	X	....	....	X	....	....
Primary-secondary coupling	X	....	....	X	X	....
Secondary implosion	X	....	....	X	X	....

CAPABILITIES NEEDED TO ENSURE HIGH CONFIDENCE IN WARHEAD SAFETY AND RELIABILITY—Continued

Weapon physics	Computer simulation	DARHT	Subcritical experiments	NIF	Pulsed power	LANSCE
Weapon performance	X					

Under the Stockpile Stewardship Program, computational modeling and numerical simulation provide the critical integration of theory, existing data, new experimental results, and predictions into results that can be verified and validated. Advanced computational capabilities (application codes, computing platforms, and various tools and techniques) are being developed under the Accelerated Strategic Computing Initiative and incorporated into ongoing stockpile computational activities. The weapons scientists and engineers will be focused on numerical simulations and experiments. The goal is to combine past nuclear test data, computational modeling, and new data from current and advanced experimental facilities to fill in knowledge gaps and extend the fundamental understanding in all vital areas.

To assess the aging-related changes that occur in the nuclear and nonnuclear warhead components, complex three-dimensional computational simulations that are beyond current computational capabilities are needed. Through the Accelerated Strategic Computing Initiative, the enhanced capabilities are being developed. For example, increases of more than ten-thousandfold in computational speed, network capacity, and data storage are planned to provide simulations of weapon safety, reliability, and performance. These efforts are closely linked to experiments to validate new and evolving computer models and to provide improved physics.

These new capabilities will be used in addition to the experimental and computational capabilities developed during the nuclear testing era. However, because these older tools were designed to complement nuclear testing, they are not, in and of themselves, sufficient in the absence of nuclear testing. As new facilities and capabilities come on line and are validated, their data will be incorporated into our assessments. This transition period should take several more years.

Peer review is a key component of stockpile stewardship. Because assessment and certification of stockpile safety, reliability, and performance rely heavily on expert judgment, it is essential that the assessment process be vetted and validated. Peer review, both formal and informal, takes place among the three weapons laboratories. In addition, periodic independent reviews by outside experts help provide confidence in the credibility of the laboratories' assessments and in the process by which the assessments are made.

Refurbishing and Recertifying: Design and Manufacturing

Nuclear warheads are not static objects. They contain radioactive materials that decay and organic materials that decompose with time. Some materials, like tritium, decay predictably and must be replaced every few years throughout the warhead's lifetime. In addition, radioactive decay produces changes in the radioactive materials themselves and in adjacent materials. For example, plastics and other organic materials change with age and exposure to heat and radiation. Many of the metals used in nuclear warheads are chemically reactive and are damaged by long-term storage and exposure to radiation. As a result, all warhead parts must be considered limited-lifetime components, and all warheads in the enduring stockpile will require periodic refurbishment and remanufacturing.

With an improved understanding of the effects of aging on warhead safety, reliability, and performance, developed through the enhanced surveillance and assessment efforts, the Department of Energy will be able to take a proactive approach to refurbishment. The goal is to replace or fix components systematically, before aging-related changes jeopardize warhead safety or performance.

The Stockpile Life Extension Process (shown graphically on the next page) provides the framework for research and development activities and production planning. To retain confidence in warhead safety, security, and performance, the SLEP risk management strategy addresses three categories of potential refurbishment actions: musts—correct known degradations; shoulds—prevent foreseeable degradations; coulds—enhance safety or security. A number of specific life extension options are being defined for each warhead type, allowing the laboratories, plants, and the Department of Defense to anticipate and plan for future maintenance and refurbishment requirements. The schedule guides stockpile-related research and development—at the laboratories to design and certify replacement components and validate new materials and at the plants to develop and certify new manufacturing processes.

A new approach to manufacturing is being implemented to fit the capacity of the downsized and consolidated production complex and make full use of its capabilities. Through the Advanced Design and Production Technology (ADAPT) initiative, the laboratories and plants are working together to:

—Integrate product and process design through the concurrent design and development of replacement components and the processes used to manufacture them.

—Develop and qualify new manufacturing processes that produce high production yields, are more efficient, and meet modern environmental, safety, and health requirements.

—Develop and characterize improved materials that are functionally equivalent to the originals.

—Develop agile manufacturing technologies that allow the production complex to gear up rapidly to produce different weapon components.

—Identify, certify, and maximize the use of commercial parts and processes.

The Department of Energy will continue to meet the day-to-day production requirements for limited-lifetime component exchanges and other replacement components while also continuing to implement the Advanced Design and Production Technology initiative. For example, tritium-containing components must be replaced every few years, and various other parts are needed to reassemble warheads that are removed from the stockpile for routine surveillance and inspection.

Simulation and Modeling: Strategic Computing and Simulation

Strategic Computing and Simulation is focused on achieving capabilities needed to support the Comprehensive Test Ban Treaty and to implement the Stockpile Stewardship Plan. Currently, there are five major thrusts:

—Accelerated Strategic Computing Initiative (ASCI)

—Stockpile Computing

—Distanced Computing and Distributed Computing for Weapon Simulation (DisCom2)

—Numeric Environment for Weapon Simulations (NEWS)

—Validation and Verification (V&V)

ASCI provides the leading-edge, high-end simulation capabilities needed to meet weapon assessment and certification requirements without nuclear testing. To accomplish this, ASCI integrates the resources of the national laboratories, computer manufacturers, and academia.

The national laboratories are focused to provide the application codes and related science needed to address weapon safety, reliability, and performance without nuclear testing. They are also developing improved tools and methodologies to utilize this unprecedented volume of data. This involves research and development in the areas of security, extremely high bandwidth transmission, extremely high data rate speeds, and high-fidelity, high-density visualization of dynamic data flows. Even at this early stage in their development, advanced ASCI simulation codes are providing unprecedented capabilities to the weapons program. We are not only doing the same things faster, but performing calculations and simulations that were impossible to contemplate before.

The computer manufacturers are developing the technology and systems needed to operate at 1, 3, 10, 30, and 100 trillion operations per second. This technology is being developed at about twice the rate of commercial advances. ASCI has been highly successful in meeting its milestones and providing highly effective new tools to support stockpile stewardship.

This unprecedented computational power is also being made available to the university community through the Academic Strategic Alliances Initiative. Five universities have received initial research awards to investigate projects in such areas as turbulence and shock physics, astrophysical thermonuclear flashes, and numerical simulation of accidental explosions. This research will have stockpile stewardship, basic science, and civilian applications.

Stockpile Computing provides weapons designers and analysts with computer center operations, model development, and code maintenance services necessary to support the current Stockpile Stewardship Program (SSP) activities. In particular, Stockpile Computing supports the surveillance, maintenance, refurbishment, assessment, and certification of the existing nuclear weapons stockpile by incremental upgrades to models and computing systems, and infusion of ASCI-proven technologies into routine SSP operations.

Stockpile Stewardship utilizes a diverse and distributed complex of facilities to maintain the safety, reliability, and performance of the nation's nuclear weapons.

DisCom2 develops and provides the technology needed to deploy an integrated environment that permits the weapons laboratories and production plants to access computing (from desktop to teraops) across thousands of miles. For example, DisCom2 provides for rapid, secure, and verified transmission of engineering design and change information between laboratory scientists and production plant engineers, enabling teams to work on a common problem in real time, simultaneously, with effective visualization and the ability to make adjustments at a distance.

There is a critical need to upgrade the information architecture at the laboratories to make effective use of ASCI teraops computers. NEWS will provide a local computational environment for large numbers of designers and analysts to use high-end simulation capabilities to simultaneously address time-urgent stockpile issues. NEWS upgrades to data archive, network, off-line processor, and visualization capabilities link ASCI computational resources to designers' and analysts' desktops to allow efficient and productive access to limited teraops computer resources.

In addition to replacing and enhancing previous test-based capabilities, there is also a need to demonstrate that the new tools are providing the correct results. V&V provides the tools, methodologies, and data to ensure that the high-end simulation capabilities accurately model physical phenomena. The Department of Energy will be able to demonstrate in many cases that the complex simulations for national security reasons are reliable, that is, have been verified and validated. Reliability is established by external use of comparable codes, applications, and other methods by the oil industry, the academic astrophysics community, and others.

Confidence in the System: Integrated Program Management

The Stockpile Stewardship Program is an integrated set of activities performed by an integrated complex of laboratories and plants. The technical challenges involved, combined with the downsizing of the production complex and the consolidation of activities at the laboratories, create the need for seamless, effective, and efficient program management. Indeed, program management lies at the heart of the new paradigm for stockpile stewardship.

The laboratories and plants are collaborating with each other and with U.S. industry to develop tritium production technologies as well as enhanced surveillance, advanced manufacturing, and computational simulation and modeling capabilities. Once the capabilities are developed and validated, integration and collaboration will continue as surveillance results are evaluated, replacement parts and manufacturing processes are designed concurrently, and refurbished warheads and components are certified.

An essential element of maintaining confidence in the stockpile—and in the system that maintains the stockpile—is the informed and vigorous interactions that take place among the laboratories, the Department of Energy, and the Department of Defense and its advisory groups. These include:

—*Peer review.*—In scientific research, peer interaction and review are essential for maintaining excellence and providing confidence in the quality of the work. In the absence of nuclear testing, the need for peer review in stockpile stewardship is greater than ever before. Vital peer interactions take place through integrated and collaborative activities among the laboratories and through formal reviews of independent activities.

—*Dual revalidation.*—This formal review process was developed in consultation with the Department of Defense. Teams from the three weapons laboratories, Los Alamos, Livermore, and Sandia—New Mexico and California—independently evaluate the safety and reliability of each warhead. The teams independently review existing calculations and experiments pertaining to the warhead, evaluate relevant stockpile surveillance results and predictive analyses, and perform separate experimental and calculational activities to investigate issues of concern and improve the baseline of understanding. Dual revalidation will be applied to all stockpile warheads, beginning with the W76. The W76 Dual Revalidation is expected to be 2 to 3 years in duration. Upon completion, the DOE and DOD will select the next weapon system for dual revalidation.

—*Stockpile Life Extension Process (SLEP).*—The Stockpile Life Extension Process addresses the need to extend the lifetime of existing warheads. It is designed to balance the concern that aging-related changes will degrade warhead safety or reliability against the concern that stockpile modifications may introduce new uncertainties. Life extension options have been defined for each warhead type in the stockpile. These refurbishments also provide the opportunity, when the warheads are disassembled, to make modifications to improve safety, reliability, or longevity. All stockpile life extension activities are closely coordinated with the Department of Defense before they are initiated.

—*Annual certification.*—The Secretary of Energy and Secretary of Defense formally certify to the President that nuclear testing is not required to assure that the U.S. nuclear stockpile is safe and reliable. This certification is based on rigorous technical analyses that lead to formal concurrence by the Nuclear Weapons Council, the Directors of the three nuclear weapons laboratories, and the Commander in Chief of the U.S. Strategic Command.

Other important interactions take place between the Department of Defense and the Department of Energy on issues related to stockpile safety and security. In addition, the Nuclear Weapons Council carries out executive decisions on stockpile actions. The Nuclear Weapons Council, which is supported by a highly specialized staff of military officers, members of the Office of the Secretary of Defense, and the Department of Energy's Assistant Secretary for Defense Programs, also reviews and coordinates the Department of Energy's stockpile plans.

STOCKPILE STEWARDSHIP PROGRAM ACCOMPLISHMENTS

More than five years have passed since the last U.S. nuclear test and more than six years since the last new warhead entered the U.S. stockpile. The decision to end nuclear testing and the absence of requirements for production of new warhead designs significantly changed the way in which the U.S. maintains the safety and reliability of its nuclear weapons stockpile. As the accomplishments highlighted below illustrate, much progress has been made in the development and successful implementation of the Stockpile Stewardship Program (SSP).

Program Architecture: The PEIS

Beginning in May 1995, the Department of Energy held a series of open-to-the-public meetings as part of the process for preparing the Programmatic Environmental Impact Statement (PEIS) for the Stockpile Stewardship Program. Meetings were held at each laboratory and plant site and in Washington, D.C. The comments, questions, and discussions arising from these meetings provided extremely useful input for refining the program.

The Record of Decision for the PEIS was signed by the Secretary of Energy on December 19, 1996. This document formally defines the architecture of the weapons complex for the Stockpile Stewardship Program. It covers the future capabilities required of the three weapons laboratories, the four plants, and the Nevada Test Site. It calls for construction of several advanced experimental facilities at the laboratories, for downsizing production capabilities in place, and for reestablishing some manufacturing capabilities at the laboratories.

The weapons complex outlined in the PEIS is consistent with the reduced U.S. nuclear weapons stockpile under current and projected START options. It also supports the U.S. nuclear weapons policy of "lead plus hedge," as set forth in the Nuclear Posture Review (conducted by the Department of Defense and approved by the President in September 1994). With this complex, the U.S. will be able to maintain a reduced nuclear arsenal while sustaining the capabilities needed to reverse course (in terms of stockpile size, nuclear testing, and new-design warhead production), should future circumstances dictate.

Implementation Plan: The Green Book

The laboratories and plants have worked with the Department of Energy to develop a detailed implementation strategy for the Stockpile Stewardship Program. This strategy is presented in The Stockpile Stewardship and Management Plan, often referred to as the Green Book. Specific roles and responsibilities have been defined and unique facilities and capabilities identified. As the program has evolved, the strategy has been revised and modified. With an up-to-date and detailed implementation plan, jointly prepared and agreed to by the plants and laboratories, we will be able to execute the Stockpile Stewardship Program efficiently and cost effectively without gaps in necessary capabilities.

Administration and Congressional Support: The Budget

As the President has stated, "In order for this program to succeed, both the Administration and the Congress must provide sustained bipartisan support for the stockpile stewardship program over the next decade and beyond. I am committed to working with the Congress to ensure this support." The President's 1999 budget request will include a five-year plan that meets this commitment. With such budgetary support, the Department of Energy is maintaining confidence in the stockpile while proceeding with the design and construction of vital new experimental facilities and with the acquisition of the next-generation supercomputers required for the Stockpile Stewardship Program.

Confidence in the Stockpile: The Annual Certification

A primary responsibility of the Department of Energy is to certify the safety and reliability of the nation's nuclear weapons stockpile. Stockpile safety and reliability issues are continually assessed by the Department of Energy and the Los Alamos, Livermore, and Sandia laboratories. As part of the Stockpile Stewardship Program, a formal annual certification process has been established. This process incorporates technical evaluations from DOE and DOD, the Directors of the laboratories, and advice from the Commander in Chief of the Strategic Command, the laboratories' Directors, and the Nuclear Weapons Council. The certification that the stockpile is safe and reliable relies on the expert judgment of these senior officials. The first Annual Certification was completed on February 7, 1997. In their letter to the President, the Secretary of Defense and Secretary of Energy stated that they judge the stockpile to be safe and reliable and that there is no need to conduct an underground nuclear test. The second annual certification process is under way and on schedule.

NEW CAPABILITIES

Major strides in the development and application of new capabilities to improve stockpile stewardship have been made. Data and information from these new capabilities will be integrated with data from experiments in existing facilities and from past experiments and nuclear tests. Restoration of tritium production is essential and the development of all the new experimental facilities and capabilities are needed to provide confidence in the safety, reliability, and performance of the U.S. nuclear stockpile, now and in the future.

Decisions: DARHT, NIF, Subcritical Experiments, and Tritium Production

Important decisions were reached regarding two vital new experimental facilities, subcritical experiments, and tritium production.

—*DARHT*.—The Environmental Impact Statement for the Dual-Axis Radiographic Hydrodynamic Test (DARHT) Facility was completed, and construction is under way at Los Alamos. When completed, DARHT will be the nation's most advanced facility for hydrodynamic experiments. These experiments are essential for validating the implosion performance of primaries.

—*NIF*.—Lawrence Livermore was selected as the site for the National Ignition Facility (NIF). Engineering design work is under way, and ground was broken for construction on May 29, 1997. This immense laser facility will provide a means for experimentally studying primary boosting. It will also provide important data for assessing secondary performance and weapon effects and for improving and validating new physics models and computer codes.

The Department of Energy is also investigating the feasibility of follow-on facilities that may provide additional capabilities to verify and validate the improved simulation models discussed above. To assist in the evaluation of primaries, the Advanced Hydrotest Facility (AHF) is being studied to provide improved understanding of the effects of aging and weaponization features. AHF would expand multipulse, multiaxis radiographic capabilities well beyond those planned for DARHT. To assist in the evaluation of secondaries, a proposed follow-on pulsed-power facility is being studied to extend the range of capabilities for large-scale radiation flow measurements in complex geometries. This builds upon the recent and significant advances in pulsed power resulting from modification of an existing accelerator facility at Sandia National Laboratories. Research on the technology for these facilities is in progress.

—*Subcritical Experiments*.—In April 1997, the Secretary of Energy announced a schedule for subcritical experiments, an essential component of the Stockpile Stewardship Program. The first and second subcritical experiments, "Rebound" and "Holog," were successfully completed at the Nevada Test Site on July 2 and September 18, 1997, respectively. These experiments are providing valuable scientific information about the behavior of nuclear materials during the implosion phase of warhead operation. This information is needed to accurately predict the performance of stockpile warheads as they age.

—*Tritium*.—The Department of Energy is pursuing a dual-track production strategy for the most promising tritium supply alternatives: (1) to initiate the purchase of an existing commercial reactor (operating or partially complete) or irradiation services with an option to purchase the reactor for conversion to a defense facility and (2) to design, build, and test critical components of an accelerator system for tritium production. By late 1998, the Department of Energy plans to select one of the tracks to serve as the primary source of tritium. The other alternative, if feasible, would be developed as a backup tritium source.

Substantial progress has been made for both alternatives since the announcement of the dual-track strategy.

For the Commercial Light Water Reactor Project track: (1) completed and certified the design of Tritium Producing Burnable Absorber Rods, fabricated thirty-two rods, and placed them in the Watts Bar commercial reactor for an 18-month irradiation cycle, (2) the Conceptual Design Report for the Tritium Extraction Facility was completed, independently validated, and issued, and (3) prepared and issued a Request for Proposals from nuclear utilities to sell the Department of Energy a reactor or irradiation services for tritium production. Proposals have been received and are being considered.

For the Accelerator Production of Tritium Project track: (1) the Conceptual Design Report was completed, independently validated, and issued; (2) high-power density irradiation of target/blanket materials was completed; (3) superconducting radio-frequency linear accelerator technology was adopted; and, (4) implementation of a modular approach that allows production flexibility should future tritium requirements change was initiated.

Strategic Computing and Simulation Advances: Entering the Teraops Era

Industry has begun delivering the advanced new computers required for ASCI. ASCI's goal is to develop the complex three-dimensional models of weapons operation needed to make the integrated simulations that will provide a digital proxy for nuclear testing as well as provide capabilities needed to address aging and other emerging issues. Intel Corp. and Sandia National Laboratories are working in partnership on the ASCI Red machine, in which thousands of Pentium processors are linked together using a technique known as massively parallel processing. In December 1996, the machine demonstrated record-breaking teraop operation, performing one trillion operations in a second, which made headlines around the world. The system will eventually be made up of more than 9,000 processors and will be able to operate at 1.4 teraops.

IBM and Lawrence Livermore National Laboratory are developing the ASCI Blue Pacific machine. Los Alamos National Laboratory and SGI/Cray are developing the ASCI Blue Mountain machine. Both systems are intended to achieve benchmark performance at or above 3 trillion operations per second. At this early stage in their development, advanced ASCI weapons simulation codes are providing unprecedented capabilities to the weapons scientists and engineers. For example, coupled three-dimensional thermal-chemical-hydrodynamic calculations of weapon safety (for example, a weapon in a fire) are now possible. As a practical matter, some standard weapons-related calculations have been performed one hundred times faster than before. Through this initiative, the time it took to run one simulation was reduced from 74 days to 7 hours.

In July 1997, Secretary Peña announced research awards to five major U.S. universities—Stanford University, California Institute of Technology, the University of Chicago, the University of Utah at Salt Lake, and the University of Illinois at Urbana/Champaign. These universities will collaborate with the Los Alamos, Lawrence Livermore, and Sandia National Laboratories on challenging projects that will drive the advancement of large-scale computational modeling.

MEETING THE DAY-TO-DAY NEEDS OF THE STOCKPILE

The Department of Energy has continued to maintain the U.S. nuclear weapons stockpile. Problems in the stockpile have arisen since the cessation of nuclear testing. Some of these problems are similar to those for which, in the past, nuclear tests were conducted to investigate or resolve. However, using the stockpile stewardship approach, we are drawing on test-related expertise and on emerging new capabilities to evaluate and resolve these problems.

Dual Revalidation: The W76

The W76 dual revalidation is prototyping this formal process for certifying a warhead's conformance with its military characteristics, and obtaining a thorough baseline condition of the weapon. Two separate teams of experts from the weapons laboratories are independently assessing the warhead and combining new computational and experimental investigations with stockpile surveillance results, predictive analyses, and data from past nuclear and nonnuclear tests.

Stockpile Life Extension Process: The W87

The W87 life extension process incorporates changes to enhance the structural integrity of the warhead. Engineering development is proceeding and includes above ground experiments high-fidelity flight testing. The effect of the proposed design changes on the warhead's performance is being assessed using the latest computational models, supported by the existing nuclear and nonnuclear test database and laboratory experiments. Experience gained in the W87 refurbishment will guide future life extension activities for other stockpile warheads.

New Process Qualification: Gas Reservoirs at Kansas City

Production of tritium gas reservoirs was moved from the Rocky Flats Plant to the Kansas City Plant. Kansas City is now responsible for manufacturing gas reservoirs for all warheads in the enduring stockpile. Development and qualification of the production processes are under way. This past year, the gas reservoir production programs for two warhead systems—the W76 and the W80—were qualified.

Qualification of this critical production capability demonstrates that the risks inherent in consolidating and downsizing the production complex can be successfully managed and mitigated.

New Production Capability: Neutron Generators at Sandia

The production responsibility for neutron generators has been successfully transferred from the Pinellas Plant to Sandia-New Mexico. The new production facility was dedicated in July 1996, and approximately 364 units will be recertified in 1997. This new facility will support both production requirements and research and development for new extended-life neutron generators. In support of Sandia production efforts, Los Alamos has developed the capability for tritium loading the targets needed for the neutron tubes.

New Production Capability: Nonnuclear

Under the Nonnuclear Reconfiguration Initiative, a number of production responsibilities have been transferred from the Mound, Pinellas, and Rocky Flats plants to Los Alamos National Laboratory in addition to the Neutron Tube Target Loading assignment. The production responsibility for detonators has been successfully transferred and the capability is being installed. Los Alamos also has responsibility for producing beryllium components and nonnuclear pit parts.

Limited Pit Production Capability at Los Alamos

The responsibility for pit surveillance and pit manufacture has been transferred from the Rocky Flats Plant to Los Alamos. A pit surveillance capability has been established and pit evaluation was initiated this year. Limited pit manufacturing will now be done at Los Alamos. The first demonstration W88 replacement pit is scheduled to be produced in 1998.

Weapon Dismantlement

Dismantlement of the Cold War arsenal is being carried out as the Department of Energy continues to develop the enhanced capabilities and facilities needed to support the enduring U.S. stockpile. As a result of the START I treaty and separate Presidential decisions, thousands of weapons have been removed from the U.S. stockpile and are slated for dismantlement. More than 1,000 weapons were dismantled in 1996, and nearly 500 weapons will be dismantled in 1997.

Successful Application of the SSP Model: The B61 Mod 11

Replacement of the B53 with the B61 Mod 11 has improved the inherent safety of the U.S. stockpile. The B53 gravity bomb was the oldest weapon in the stockpile and was produced before modern safety features were developed. By modifying a small fraction of the existing B61 Mod 7 bombs, the Department of Defense can retire the B53 from the stockpile while still meeting its mission requirements.

Conversion of B61 Mod 7's to Mod 11's requires replacement of the radar nose and center case with a one-piece hardened steel nose and replacement of the parachute in the bomb's tail assembly with steel ballast parts and a drag flare to change the flight characteristics of the weapon. The Department of Energy authorized these changes in December 1995. The tail case subassembly retrofit was assigned to Kansas City and the nose case replacement to the Oak Ridge Y–12 Plant. A very tight schedule called for delivery of the first conversion kit one year later, in December 1996.

Teams from Los Alamos, Sandia-New Mexico, and the production plants addressed and defined appropriate qualification tests and analyses for certifying the acceptability of the modified bomb and its new delivery conditions. A number of successful flight tests confirmed that the modified warhead will perform as expected and can be deployed as a replacement for the B53.

Because of the tight schedule and an already heavy workload in its machining facilities, Kansas City procured a number of parts for the tail case subassembly from commercial vendors. Assembly of the modified tail case was done at Kansas City. The first conversion kit was delivered ahead of schedule, in November 1996.

The accelerated schedule presented challenges to the Oak Ridge Y–12 Plant as well, particularly because a number of critical operations had to be restarted from an extended stand-down. Numerous issues related to the replacement nose case had to be resolved during production. The first conversion kit of the replacement nose case was shipped in mid-December 1996, two weeks ahead of schedule.

The conversion of B61 Mod 7's to Mod 11's successfully demonstrated many aspects of the Stockpile Stewardship Program. Integration of design and production engineering was a key factor in meeting the tight schedule. Teamwork between the laboratories and the plants and between the plants and commercial vendors allowed the Department of Energy to deliver the modified warhead in under a year (as opposed to two to three years for a retrofit under the old paradigm). In years past, the Department of Energy would likely have conducted at least one nuclear test to validate the modified bomb. However, because nuclear-test- and design-experienced people and all necessary computer analysis and other required data were available at both the plants and the laboratories, the B61 Mod 11 could be certified and put into the stockpile without a nuclear test.

With the successful completion of the B61 Mod 11, the Department of Energy has gained experience and confidence in the Stockpile Stewardship Program. This project confirmed the value of the new approach to manufacturing. In particular, it confirmed the feasibility of stockpile modernization via retrofitting and life extension of existing warheads. It also showcased the Department of Energy's ability to respond rapidly across the entire weapons complex to an important stockpile issue.

CONCLUSION

Under the Stockpile Stewardship Program, the Department of Energy's goal is unchanged from previous years—namely, to provide high confidence in the safety, reliability, and performance of the U.S. nuclear warhead stockpile. Absent nuclear testing, the tools have changed significantly—stockpile confidence will now rely on nonnuclear demonstration-based assessments of warhead safety, reliability, and performance. New experimental and computational capabilities are being developed. With these tools, the Department of Energy must be able to mitigate the loss of critical expertise that will result from the retirement of nuclear-test- and design-experienced weapons scientists and engineers. In the coming years, we will validate these new tools, integrate the information they provide with the suite of weapons-related data and models, and train the next generation of stockpile stewards.

As previously described, taking full advantage of the capabilities of the Stockpile Stewardship Program, the aged B53 bomb was replaced with a modified B61 equipped with modern safety features, and several other weapons system problems that would have previously required a nuclear test were resolved. These major achievements and the related progress being made to develop nonnuclear experimental facilities and enhanced computational capabilities provide ample evidence that the Stockpile Stewardship Program will be successful and will enable the Department of Energy to continue to maintain high confidence in the safety, reliability, and performance of the enduring U.S. nuclear deterrent.

BACKGROUND ON PROGRAM

Dr. REIS. The Stockpile Stewardship Program began in July 1993 when President Clinton announced that he would continue the moratorium on nuclear weapons testing and seek a Comprehensive Test Ban Treaty [CTBT] for nuclear weapons, a goal that has been sought since President Eisenhower. In August 1995, President Clinton announced his intention to seek a zero yield CTBT and he included as part of his announcement six safeguards that would accompany the treaty.

The first of these was that we would conduct a science-based Stockpile Stewardship Program. The Senate START II ratification text in January 1996 also commits the United States to a robust Stockpile Stewardship Program.

President Clinton signed the CTBT in September 1996 and on September 22 of this year he submitted it to the Senate for approval. As part of that submission, the administration committed to fund stockpile stewardship at about $4.5 billion in fiscal year

1999 and to use the fiscal year 1999 as a baseline for future funding. This does not include funding for construction of a new tritium production source. Thus, stockpile stewardship, which is essential to maintain our nuclear deterrent, also underpins the Nation's nuclear arms control policy.

As President Clinton stated in August 1995,

> I am assured by the Secretary of Energy and the Directors of our nuclear weapons laboratories that we can meet the challenge of maintaining our nuclear deterrent under a Comprehensive Test Ban Treaty through a science-based Stockpile Stewardship Program without nuclear testing.

Thus, Mr. Chairman, within the U.S. national security framework, the specific task of stockpile stewardship is to maintain high confidence in the safety, reliability, and performance of our nuclear stockpile indefinitely and without nuclear testing. Part of this task is to maintain the capability to return to testing and production of new weapons if so directed by the President and the Congress.

STOCKPILE STEWARDSHIP—CONCEPT AND RISKS

So what is the program, what are the risks involved, and how do we plan to mitigate those risks?

The stockpile stewardship concept is simple. Each year, representative samples of each weapon type are returned from the active forces to the plants and labs, disassembled, examined, tested and analyzed for defects—much as you would go for an annual physical or take your car to a local automobile mechanic. If any defects are found, their effect on performance, safety, and reliability is assessed and if that effect is deemed significant, the defective part is remanufactured and replaced. It's like the battery or spark plugs in your car. Some parts we know will require replacement and these are replaced at regular intervals. That's it. Sounds simple enough.

Unfortunately, while a modern nuclear weapon has about as many parts as a modern automobile, it is much more complicated. Many of the parts of a nuclear weapon are made from very special materials—plutonium, highly enriched uranium, tritium—which radioactively decay and change both their properties and the properties of other materials within the weapon.

Nuclear weapons are designed and manufactured to extraordinarily rigid standards, both to enable huge amounts of explosive energy to be packaged in relatively small containers and to maintain phenomenal safety standards. A nuclear weapon less than the size of a small desk can have the explosive power to completely destroy a modern city. And yet, it must be able to survive the worst kind of accident you can think of with less than a one in a million chance of exploding. This level of performance and safety must be maintained throughout the weapon's lifetime, even as it ages and changes.

While we can expect the aging will cause the defect rate to rise, just as it does with both humans and cars, we cannot go out and buy a new warhead model. There is no new warhead production and some of the old factories are out of business. Moreover, the weapons designers who have had the experience with nuclear explosive testing are also aging. In about 10 years, most of them will have been retired. This means that about the same time the weapons reach the end of their design life, we will no longer have anyone on the job with direct test experience.

Despite these challenges, people from the weapons laboratories, the production plants, and the Federal establishment involved in stockpile stewardship have testified and will so testify that we can do the stockpile stewardship job. We believe we can maintain the safety and reliability of the nuclear weapons in the stockpile indefinitely without underground testing and keep the risks to manageable levels.

How do we expect to do this? First of all, we start from a solid position. The current stockpile has been well tested, is in very good shape, and is well understood. We have an extensive database on each of these weapons and we have a cadre of experienced designers, engineers, scientists and technicians that can, with confidence, certify the safety and reliability of the current stockpile.

Now since we cannot do a complete test of a nuclear explosion, we conceptually divide the explosion into each of its parts and test and analyze each of these separately, much as you would test the ignition system, the cooling system, and the brakes of your car. Then we put the whole thing together into a computer calculation, a simulation to see if the resulting performance is within specification. Each part of the simulation must predict the results of each of the separate tests and where they exist must be consistent with data from previous underground nuclear tests. Let me give you some very simplified examples of how this works.

Some of the processes are relatively straight forward to simulate. The first part of the nuclear explosion sequence is to send the right electrical signal to the right place at the right time. We can test this exactly by flight testing actual weapons with inert mockups of nuclear components. We can do a good job of testing the first part of the nuclear explosion, the implosion of the plutonium pit. But we do not use actual plutonium. It would go off if we did. Then we can measure a number of important features by taking x-ray pictures during critical parts of the experiment. We can then compare these pictures with calculations and previous actual underground nuclear test results.

EXPERIMENTAL AND DIAGNOSTIC TOOLS

But current radiographic systems will not be sufficient to measure the effects of potential defects in aged pits, so we are building a new x-ray machine, the dual-axis radiographic hydrodynamic test [DARHT], which will look at the shape and size of an imploding pit model from two different directions and with much better resolution.

Beyond obtaining x-ray pictures of imploding pit models, however, we will no longer experimentally simulate a nuclear explosion, but instead, will use experimental facilities to obtain conditions that occur during such an explosion and then use the results of these experiments to check computer calculations. For example, we are investigating the way old plutonium behaves when subjected to high pressures of an implosion to subcritical tests at the Nevada test site, and we expect to be able to generate conditions of temperature and pressure of nuclear explosions with lasers at the national ignition facility. These and other experimental facilities that are online, under construction, or in the planning stage, will give us a set of tools sufficient to investigate and help understand anticipated problems in the stockpile.

As I mentioned previously, the experimental information is tied to the assessment process through computation or, more precisely, numerical simulation. But we know that the level of computation needed to effectively simulate effects of aging or a remanufactured part is much, much greater than that which is currently available. So we have begun a computational development program, the accelerated strategic computing initiative in parallel with the experimental program. There is no point in doing elegant experiments if you cannot interpret the results in terms of nuclear weapon safety and reliability, and there is no point in doing simulations if the computer codes cannot be grounded in reality. You need both as well as returning to the archives to match the new techniques with the data from the underground nuclear tests.

It is this troika of computer simulation, experiments, and previous nuclear test data that provides us a complete tool box for the assessment process. Building this assessment tool box in time to train the new cadre of scientists and engineers is critical to the Stockpile Stewardship Program.

WEAPON REMANUFACTURE

This leaves remanufacture. We know now we will have to remanufacture and replace some parts and are already doing so. We know that eventually we will have to replace just about every part in just about every weapon. That is the whole idea of stockpile life extension. But to create these new parts, we cannot rely on the cold war production complex that has produced some tens of thousands of nuclear weapons. We are establishing a production complex that is much more flexible and much more environmentally sensitive than the production complex it replaces.

We must use every applicable modern manufacturing technique, the best that U.S. industry can offer. We must understand the details of the manufacturing processes with sufficient precision so as not to introduce new defects into a remanufactured system. The key here is model based manufacturing, similar to that which created the Boeing 777 and being applied today by much of U.S. industry. Thus, around one-half of the stewardship program is devoted to producing current replacement parts and to planning and modernizing our production complex to match the new job. We envision a complex that is approximately one-fifth the size of the cold war complex but one that can return to higher levels of production if the need ever arises.

While we do not expect to need additional supplies of enriched uranium and plutonium, there is one nuclear material which we know we have to produce—tritium, a radioactive isotope of hydrogen that is required for every modern nuclear weapon.

Tritium decays fairly rapidly. Approximately 5 percent is transformed to helium every year. The last tritium that was produced in the United States was in 1988. With the end of the cold war and with the reduction of numbers of nuclear weapons, we have had large amounts of excess tritium. This excess has been used to make up for the decayed tritium in the current stockpile. But eventually this will run out. Based upon our current estimates, we must produce tritium by the year 2005 to support a START I nuclear stockpile. After a number of years of analysis and changing requirements, we are down to two approaches for making tritium—using an existing commercial light water reactor or using a newly developed accelerator. The DOE will select a primary source for tritium production as soon as possible in fiscal year 1998.

So, in a nutshell, that is stockpile stewardship—maintaining the stockpile without testing, surveillance, assessment, remanufacture, tritium, labs, plants—a program that must develop a new generation of technical experts before the current generation expires.

CHALLENGES AND RISKS

Why do we think we can manage this challenge and what can we do to manage the risks?

First, let me reiterate that we start from a solid base. The current stockpile is well tested and well understood. The designers and engineers who built them are available and active and, indeed, they are the ones who are creating the Stockpile Stewardship Program. They are the ones who are working on the stockpile now and are helping to train their successors.

Second, we have laid out a plan for the Stockpile Stewardship Program—weapon by weapon, part by part—that projects the tasks that are required to maintain the stockpile over the next 10 years and beyond. We have concurrence on this program from the Department of Defense and the Joint Chiefs and the administration has committed to fund this program and all its parts.

Third, as one of the conditions for ratification, Safeguard F, the President requires us to annually certify to him directly the safety, reliability, and the performance of each weapon type. This is done by the Secretary of Defense and the Secretary of Energy on the advice of the Nuclear Weapons Council, the directors of the nuclear weapons laboratories, and the commander in chief of the Strategic Command. As you recall, Secretary Peña went through that with you in some detail.

Fourth, we have a backup, safeguard C requires us to maintain the Nevada test site in a state of readiness, and the subcritical and other experiments conducted there help keep the people sharp and ready.

Fifth, safeguard B states that the ratification is conditioned on maintaining the vitality of the nuclear weapons laboratories—Los Alamos, Lawrence Livermore, and Sandia National Laboratories. Mr. Chairman, those labs are among the best in the world and, in my opinion, they are the best in the world. And they are better now than they were 4 years ago because of the enthusiasm and vigor with which they are attacking the Stockpile Stewardship Program. History tells us that great labs need great missions and stewardship is just such a mission. Our DOE labs will get even better because they will attract the kind of people who are drawn to solve tough problems of national importance.

Sixth, we are doing stewardship now and doing it successfully. It has been 5 years since the last underground nuclear test. We are just completing our second annual certification. We have modified the B–61 bomb and have seen it enter the stockpile to replace the aged B–53 bomb. We have initiated a number of new experimental tools and our computation program has developed the world's fastest super computer by a factor of three. We have solved some problems by using stewardship tools that in the past would have likely required nuclear testing. We have literally done hundreds of experiments that increase our understanding of nuclear weapons. We have safely dismantled over 9,000 nuclear weapons since the end of the cold war and have produced numerous parts on time while continuing to downsize the complex. This is a system that works and not just at the labs but also at the plants—Oak Ridge Y–12, Pantex, Kansas City, Savannah River, and the Nevada test site.

So let me finish by getting to the essential question: Do I have the confidence that the Stockpile Stewardship Program will work and can we maintain the nuclear weapons stockpile without testing 10, 20, or 30 years from now?

My answer now is an almost unqualified yes.

The source of my optimism lies not in the immortality of the current stockpile of weapons, though, in truth, they are truly technological marvels, but in my faith in the integrity, courage, and competence of the people in our weapons labs and production complex. They are the men and women that designed and produced the weapons that ended World War II and kept the cold war cold. They have put together a program that is comprehensive, coherent, and robust. They believe and I believe that they can do the job by first and foremost maintaining and supporting the institutions to do that job. I have confidence in them, their integrity, their competence, and their overriding dedication to their mission. If we give them the tools that they need and stick with it, we can manage the risks.

PREPARED STATEMENT

In the end, this is not an issue of technology, but an issue of courage and will and persistence. If we have the courage and will and persistence, we will not fail.

I thank you, Mr. Chairman, and I would be glad to answer any of your questions.

[The statement follows:]

PREPARED STATEMENT OF VICTOR H. REIS

Thank you, Mr Chairman for the opportunity to testify before you today on the Stockpile Stewardship Program. This program is fundamental to our national security under a Comprehensive Test Ban Treaty. I'd like to begin with a brief history of stockpile stewardship, state what it is, give you its current status, and then answer your questions. In addition to my written testimony, I would like to provide the subcommittee with a recently published overview on the program, and if you wish, submit it for the record.

The Stockpile Stewardship program began in July 1993 when President Clinton announced he would continue the moratorium on nuclear weapons testing and seek a comprehensive test ban treaty for nuclear weapons, a goal that has been sought since President Eisenhower. In August of 1995 President Clinton announced his intention to seek a "zero yield" CTBT. He included as part of his announcement, six safeguards that would accompany the treaty. The first of these was that we will conduct a "science based stockpile stewardship program." The Senate Start II ratification text in January 1996 also commits the U.S. to a "robust Stockpile Stewardship Program."

President Clinton signed the CTBT in September of 1996, and on September 22 of this year he submitted it to the Senate for approval. As part of the submission, the Administration committed to fund stockpile stewardship at about $4.5 billion in fiscal year 1999 and to use fiscal year 1999 as a baseline for future funding. This does not include funding for construction of a new tritium production source. Thus, stockpile stewardship—which is essential to maintain our nuclear deterrent—also underpins the nation's nuclear arms control policy.

As President Clinton stated in August of 1995: "I am assured by the Secretary of Energy and the Directors of our nuclear weapons labs that we can meet the challenge of maintaining our nuclear deterrent under a Comprehensive Test Ban Treaty through a science based stockpile stewardship program without nuclear testing."

Thus, Mr. Chairman, within the U.S. national security framework, the specific task of stockpile stewardship is to maintain high confidence in the safety, reliability, and performance of the nuclear stockpile, indefinitely, without nuclear testing. And part of this task is to maintain the capability to return to testing and production of new weapons, if so directed by the President and the Congress.

So, what is the program, what are the risks involved, and how do we plan to mitigate those risks?

The stockpile stewardship concept is simple. Each year representative samples of each type of weapon are returned from the active forces to the plants and labs, disassembled, examined, tested and analyzed for defects, much as you would go for an annual physical or take your car into your local automobile mechanic. If any defects are found, their effect on performance, safety, and reliability is assessed, and if that effect is deemed significant, the defective part is remanufactured and replaced. Like the battery or spark plugs in your car, some parts we know will require replacement, and these are replaced at regular intervals. That's it. It sounds simple enough.

Unfortunately, while a modern nuclear weapon has about as many parts as a modern automobile, it is much more complicated. Many of the parts of a nuclear weapon are made from very special materials—plutonium, enriched uranium, tritium—which radioactively decay, and change both their properties and the properties of other materials within the weapon.

Nuclear weapons are designed and manufactured to extraordinarily rigid standards, both to enable huge amounts of explosive energy to be packaged in relatively small containers, and to maintain phenomenal safety standards. A nuclear weapon, less than the size of a small desk, will have the explosive power to completely destroy a modern city, and yet it must be able to survive the worst kind of accident you can think of with less than a one in a million chance of exploding. This level of performance and safety must be maintained throughout the weapon's lifetime, even as it ages and changes.

While we can expect that aging will cause the defect rate to rise—just like it does in both humans and cars—we can't go out and buy a new warhead model—there is no new warhead production, and some of the old factories are out of business. Moreover, the weapons designers who have had experience with nuclear explosive testing are also aging, in about ten years most of them will have retired. This means that about the same time all of the weapons reach the end of their design life, we will no longer have anyone on the job with direct test experience!

Despite these challenges, people from the weapons laboratories, the production plants, and the federal establishment involved in stockpile stewardship have testified, and will so testify, that we can do the stockpile stewardship job. We believe we can maintain the safety and reliability of the nuclear weapons in the stockpile indefinitely without underground testing and keep the risks to manageable levels.

How do we expect to do this?

First of all, we start from a solid position. The current stockpile has been well tested, is in very good shape and is well understood. We have an extensive data base on each of these weapons, and we have a cadre of experienced designers, engineers, scientists, and technicians that can, with confidence, certify the safety and reliability of the current stockpile.

Now, since we cannot do a complete test of a nuclear explosion, we conceptually divide the explosion into each of its parts and test and analyze each of these separately, much as you would test the ignition system, the cooling system, and the brakes on your car. We then put the whole thing together into a computer calculation—a simulation—to see if the resulting performance is within its specification. Each part of the simulation must predict the results of each of the separate tests, and where they exist, be consistent with data from previous underground nuclear tests. Let me give you some very simplified examples of how this works.

Some of processes are relatively straight forward to simulate. The first part of the nuclear explosion sequence is to send the right electrical signal to the right place at the right time. We can test this exactly by flight testing actual weapons with inert mockups of the nuclear components.

We can do a good job of testing the first part of the nuclear explosion, the implosion of the plutonium pit, but we do not use actual plutonium—it would go off if we did—and we can measure a number of important features by taking x-ray pictures during critical parts of the experiment. We can then compare these pictures with calculations and with previous actual underground nuclear test results. But current radiographic systems will not be sufficient to measure the effects of potential defects in an aged pit, so we are building a new x-ray machine—the DARHT—which will look at the shape and size of an imploding pit model from two different directions and with much better resolution.

Beyond obtaining x-ray pictures of imploding pit models, however, we will no longer experimentally simulate a nuclear explosion, but instead use experimental facilities to obtain conditions that occur during such an explosion and then use the results of these experiments to check computer calculations. For example, we are investigating the way old plutonium behaves when subjected to the high pressures of an implosion, through subcritical tests at the Nevada Test Site, and we expect to be able to generate the conditions of temperature and pressure of nuclear explosions with lasers at the National Ignition Facility. These, and other experimental facilities that are on line, under construction, or in the planning stage, will give us a set of tools sufficient to investigate and help understand anticipated problems in the stockpile.

As I mentioned previously the experimental information is tied into the assessment process through computation, or more precisely, numerical simulation. But we know that the level of computation needed to effectively simulate effects of aging or a remanufactured part is much, much greater than that currently available, so we have begun a computation development program—the Accelerated Strategic Computing Initiative—in parallel with the experimental program. There is no point in doing elegant experiments if you can't interpret the results in terms of nuclear weapons safety and reliability, and there is no point in doing simulations if the computer codes cannot be grounded in reality. You need both, as well as returning to the archives to match the new techniques with the data from underground nuclear tests. It is this troika of computer simulation, experiments, and previous nuclear test data that provides the complete tool box for the assessment process. Building this assessment "tool box" in time to train the new cadre of scientists and engineers is critical to the stockpile stewardship program.

This leaves remanufacture—we know now we will have to remanufacture and replace some parts, and are already doing so. We know that eventually we will have to replace just about every part in every weapon—that's the idea of stockpile life extension. But to create these new parts we cannot rely on the cold war production complex that produced some tens of thousands of nuclear weapons. We are establishing a production complex that is much smaller, more flexible, and much more environmentally sensitive than the production complex it replaces.

We must use every applicable modern manufacturing technique; the best that U.S. industry can offer. We must understand the details of the manufacturing processes with sufficient precision, so as not to introduce new defects into a remanufactured system. The key here is model—based manufacturing—similar to that which created the Boeing 777 and is being applied today by much of U.S. industry. Thus, around half of the stewardship program is devoted to producing current replacement parts, and to planning and modernizing our production complex to match the new job. We envision a complex of approximately one-fifth the size of the cold war complex, but one that can return to higher levels of production if the need ever arises.

While we do not expect to need additional supplies of enriched uranium and plutonium, there is one nuclear material which we know we will have to produce: tritium—a radioactive isotope of hydrogen that is required for every modern nuclear weapon.

Tritium decays fairly rapidly; approximately 5 percent is transformed to helium every year. The last tritium that was produced in the U.S. was in 1988, but with the end of the cold war and the reduction of numbers of nuclear weapons, we have had large amounts of excess tritium. This excess has been used to make up for the decayed tritium in the current stockpile, but eventually this will run out. Based upon current estimates we must produce tritium by 2005 to support a START I nuclear stockpile. After a number of years of analysis and changing requirements we are down to two approaches for making tritium—using an existing commercial light water reactor or using a newly developed accelerator. The DOE will select a primary source for tritium production as soon as possible in fiscal year 1998.

So in a nut shell, that's stockpile stewardship—maintaining the stockpile without testing—surveillance, assessment, remanufacture—tritium, labs, and plants,—a program that must develop a new generation of technical experts before the current generation retires.

Why do we think we can meet this challenge, and what are we doing to manage the risks?

First, let me reiterate that we start from a solid base. The current stockpile is well tested and well understood. The designers and engineers who built them are available and are active. Indeed they are the ones who are creating the stockpile stewardship program. They are the ones who are working on the stockpile now, and are helping to train their successors.

Second, we have laid out a plan for the stockpile stewardship program—weapon by weapon, part by part, that projects the tasks that are required to maintain the stockpile over the next ten years, and beyond. We have concurrence on this program from the Department of Defense, and the Joint Chiefs, and the administration has committed to fund this program and all its parts.

Third, as one of the conditions for ratification, Safeguard F, the President requires us to annually certify, to him directly, the safety, reliability and performance of each weapon type. This is done by the Secretary of Defense and the Secretary of Energy on the advice of the Nuclear Weapons Council, the Directors of the nuclear weapons laboratories and the Commander-in-Chief of the U.S. Strategic Command. (If a high level of confidence in the safety or reliability of a nuclear weapon type which the two Secretaries consider critical to our nuclear deterrent could no longer be certified, the President, in consultation with Congress, would be prepared to withdraw from the CTBT under the standard "supreme national interest" clause in order to conduct whatever testing might be required.)

Fourth, we have a back up. Safeguard C, requires us to maintain the Nevada Test Site in a state of readiness, and the subcritical and other experiments conducted there help keep the people sharp and ready.

Fifth, Safeguard B states that ratification is conditioned on maintaining the vitality of the nuclear weapons laboratories—Los Alamos, Lawrence Livermore and Sandia National Laboratories. Mr. Chairman, those labs are among the best in the world—in my opinion they are the best in the world—and they are better now than they were four years ago because of the enthusiasm and vigor with which they are attacking the stockpile stewardship effort. History tells us that great labs need great missions, and stewardship is just such a mission. Our DOE labs will get even better because they will attract the kind of people who are drawn to solve tough problems of national importance.

Sixth, we are doing stewardship now, and doing it successfully. It has been five years since the last underground nuclear test. We are just completing our second annual certification. We have modified the B61 bomb and seen it enter the stockpile to replace the aged B53 bomb. We have initiated a number of new experimental tools, and our computation program has developed the world's fastest supercomputer—by a factor of three. And we have solved some problems by using stewardship tools that in the past would have likely required nuclear testing. We have literally done hundreds of experiments that increase our understanding of nuclear weapons. We have safely dismantled over nine thousand nuclear weapons since the end of the Cold War, have produced numerous parts, on time, while continuing to downsize the complex. This is a system that works, and not just at the labs but also at the plants: Oak Ridge Y–12, Pantex, Kansas City, Savannah River, and the Nevada Test Site.

So let me finish by getting to the essential question: Do I have confidence that stockpile stewardship will work, can we maintain the nuclear weapon stockpile, without testing, ten, twenty, thirty years from now?

My answer now is an (almost) unqualified yes.

The source of my optimism lies not in the immortality of the current stockpile of weapons—though in truth they are truly technological marvels—but in my faith in the integrity, courage and competence of the people in our weapons labs and production complex. They are the men and women that designed and produced the weapons that ended World War II and kept the Cold War cold. They have put together a program that is comprehensive, coherent, and robust. They believe, and I believe, they can do the job, by first and foremost maintaining and supporting the institutions to do the job. I have confidence in them—their integrity, their competence, and their overriding dedication to their mission. If we give them the tools that they need, and stick with it, we can manage the risk. In the end this is not an issue of technology but an issue of courage and will and persistence, and if we have the courage and will and persistence, we will not fail.

Thank you, Mr. Chairman, and I would be glad to answer any of your questions.

Senator DOMENICI. I think if you would add to your last three words or tell me that it includes them, there must be a sense of urgency lest we get lackadaisical.

Dr. REIS. I would certainly include that. Yes.

Senator DOMENICI. When we wrap up this session, we are going right across the hall for the closed session. It should not take very long. We will just lead the witnesses over there. We will go with whomever is cleared.

Senator Reid, I am yielding to you as I did last time for your personal questions.

FUNDING FOR STOCKPILE STEWARDSHIP

Senator REID. You are very kind, Mr. Chairman.

You heard the questions that I asked Secretary Peña about the $4.5 billion, that being a bottom and not a balloon figure, and he indicated that that was the bare minimum that was needed to maintain the safety and reliability of our stockpile.

Would the three of you agree that that figure is appropriate?

Senator DOMENICI. Mr. Miller, why don't you answer first as we started today with you.

Mr. MILLER. Senator, I am on the policy side and will defer to Dr. Reis and Dr. Smith in this case.

Senator DOMENICI. All right.

Dr. Smith.

Dr. SMITH. The numbers have been carefully scrubbed. There is no question about that. As to predicting what budgets are required many years into the future, of course, I would not do that. That is why I am so pleased with the way the Nuclear Weapons Council is constructed, so that we can, indeed, year-by-year go into ever greater detail to make sure that the program is meeting what will be, one would think, changing requirements.

So I would agree with Secretary Peña that there is no fat in the budget we are currently in the process of submitting to the Congress. But I cannot agree regarding the years beyond that without further study, which, of course, is going to take time.

I can assure you, Senator Reid, that we are going to conduct the thorough studies that I just mentioned.

ANNUAL CERTIFICATION

Senator REID. The annual certification is not a political judgment, in your estimation, it is a scientific judgment? Is that true?

Dr. SMITH. That is certainly true.

Secretary Peña did a fine job in going through this chart, and the expertise from the warfighter to the scientist, from the bureaucrat to the official is, I think, quite properly and thoroughly brought to bear.

Senator REID. Secretary Reis, would you agree with that?

Dr. REIS. Yes; I would. And I would like to say, first, that I agree with Secretary Peña without qualification. I would like for that to get on the record, please.

Mr. MILLER. Senator Reid, if I might from a policy standpoint——

Senator REID. Please.

Mr. MILLER [continuing]. That is the only way we would accept the certification process. It has to be technical. It has to be based only on the science and what is observed in the stockpile.

Dr. REIS. Senator Reid, I would like to get back to the certification. We really have done an extraordinarily thorough job at this stage of the game. I think we discussed that, as you will recall, with Senator Cochran's committee as well.

I believe it was Senator Cochran or one of the people on your committee—perhaps it was Senator Levin—asked is there anybody else that we could think of, both myself and Dr. Barker, who could participate in that who is not participating, and neither of us could think of anybody. I think it has been an extraordinarily thorough process.

Again, I would like to compliment Dr. Smith, because it is under the auspices of the Nuclear Weapons Council that that process is done.

Senator REID. I have a number of other questions, Mr. Chairman, that I would ask all the panel to respond to. I also have some questions for closed session. The problem is that I have a couple of conflicts and might not be there to be able to do that.

Senator DOMENICI. Just give me your closed session questions.

Senator REID. That would be great.

Thank you very much.

Senator DOMENICI. Thank you.

Senator Cochran.

CTBT SAFEGUARDS

Senator COCHRAN. Thank you, Mr. Chairman.

Mr. Miller, you mentioned the safeguards that are associated with the Comprehensive Test Ban Treaty. I know Secretary of Energy Peña also discussed those.

In connection with safeguard F, which I understand the President has said he could use if he had been advised by the Secretaries of Energy and Defense that they were no longer confident that the nuclear weapons we had were safe and reliable, can you imagine a scenario where the secretaries would make that kind of advice available to the President?

Mr. MILLER. Yes, sir.

I do not believe it will happen. I do not believe it will happen because of the Stockpile Stewardship Program. But if the Stockpile Stewardship Program were to determine that there was a significant flaw in a weapon which played a key role in the deterrent, and that flaw could not be corrected in any other way than through a process that needed to be certified by testing, then I believe the Secretaries of Defense and Energy would come forward and I believe the President—or a President—would do exactly what the President has said safeguard F is all about.

Senator COCHRAN. It just strikes me that it is absolutely unthinkable that we would get ourselves into a position where we would announce to the world, in effect, that there were some serious flaw in our nuclear deterrent. The fact of that announcement would create such an invitation to potential enemies that it would just be unthinkable.

Mr. MILLER. If I could respond, Senator, I think the fact is that we have in this country always depended on a real deterrent and not an existential deterrent. It was not just the existence of the weapon but it was the fact that there was a weapon that had a credible means of delivery and a credible plan that backed it up, and a credible policy and a credible will that the weapons would have to be used, if necessary, that formed the entire basis of the deterrent.

If we knew ourselves that there was some terrible flaw in the system, we would owe it to the American people to fix that flaw as long as nuclear weapons were part of our security posture. I believe that we would do that.

I would say to you that, even in the circumstances that you postulate—and, again, I do not believe they are likely, but even in those circumstances—a potential enemy would not know whether that flaw would disable one of our weapons, or 12, or 100, or 500. So, if I were a potential aggressor, that would not be a sign to me that the United States was in a position of weakness. But for our own internal responsibilities, we clearly would have to come forward to the President, and the President to the Congress and to take the steps necessary as commander in chief to insure the deterrent.

Senator COCHRAN. If you had the choice of proceeding with a Stockpile Stewardship Program and testing, would you elect to do both?

Senator REID. Senator, would you repeat your question, please?

Senator COCHRAN. If you had the choice to engage in a Stockpile Stewardship Program and to test, would you do both?

Mr. MILLER. I will take the easy route and defer to my colleagues, because what we have to do here, what we have to do on the policy side is defer to the judgment of our technical experts as to the best way to maintain that stockpile. So I cannot tell you from the policy side and as a nontechnical person what the best way to maintain the stockpile is.

But Dr. Smith and Dr. Reis are more qualified to do so.

Senator COCHRAN. Dr. Smith, would you like to respond to that?

Dr. SMITH. With all deference, Senator, I do what the President tells me to do and I don't do what the President tells me not to do. He has said do not test. I do not intend to test.

Senator COCHRAN. Would withdrawal from the CTBT in your judgment be an announcement to the world that the United States has a significant problem in its nuclear stockpile?

Mr. MILLER. Sure.

Senator COCHRAN. I am going to Dr. Smith now.

Dr. SMITH. I'm afraid that would be the logical conclusion. Yes, sir.

SUPREME NATIONAL INTEREST CLAUSE

Senator COCHRAN. Dr. Smith, President Clinton has referred to the supreme national interest clause as an important feature of the CTBT. Does it make you more willing to accept the risks inherent in becoming a party to the treaty before the Stockpile Stewardship Program has proven to be a sufficient alternative to testing?

Dr. SMITH. Yes, sir.

As a scientist, I am very pleased that in extremis, which I think is very unlikely, I feel better having that escape clause, safeguard F.

CTBT SAFEGUARD C—CAPABILITY TO RESUME UNDERGROUND TESTING

Senator COCHRAN. Presidential safeguard C has also been mentioned. It says that the U.S. entry into the treaty is conditioned on the maintenance of the basic capability to resume nuclear test activities prohibited by the treaty should the United States cease to be bound to adhere to this treaty. Would it be difficult to maintain an ability to test without testing?

Dr. SMITH. I will answer briefly and then, if I may, I should defer to Dr. Reis.

I think the answer is we will be ready to test and there is good, solid evidence. We have had two truly splendid scientific experiments in the Nevada site which I think keeps the people, the equipment, and the goals up to the needs implied by further testing.

So I think yes, we are in a continual state of being able to test. Again, though, I should defer to Dr. Reis there.

DETECTION CAPABILITY

Senator COCHRAN. Let me ask you another question before Dr. Reis is given another opportunity to respond.

I understand from some technical experts that the United States has no technical means to detect tests conducted at a level of 10 kilotons or less, certainly not at the level of 1 or 2 kilotons.

Would nations like Russia and China be able to conduct testing at those levels without our being able to detect them?

Dr. SMITH. If I may, Senator, I would rather defer that answer to the closed session.

Senator COCHRAN. Secretary Reis, what is your reaction to that question that I had about safeguard C? Would it be difficult to maintain an ability to test without testing?

Dr. REIS. Senator, that is an integral part of our Stockpile Stewardship Program. The whole purpose of stewardship and the backups is also to maintain the ability to test and the ability to do production, if so desired. The examples that Dr. Smith gave I think are just right. The subcritical experiments really, I think, put everybody—pardon the expression—really to the test; you know, could they develop that type of experiment, could it be done at a particular period of time?

We also have a sufficient inventory of already drilled holes in case we have to do that. We have an inventory to get started of a number of the types of equipment we need to do that. Much of the diagnostics that we are developing now are being used on things like other type of laboratory experiments—pulsed power experiments and so forth.

So I feel that that is not something like oh, by the way. I think that is an integral part of the Stockpile Stewardship Program.

NATIONAL IGNITION FACILITY

Senator COCHRAN. Mr. Chairman, my last question is about the national ignition facility, which we discussed in our hearings in the Governmental Affairs Committee. It is one of the key elements of the Stockpile Stewardship Program. There was a predecessor program or one similar to it called NOVA, which took several years to build, and it was not until that was completely built and the switch turned on, in effect, that you found NOVA was not working. It took an additional 2 years to get it to work right.

With that experience in mind, how do you know when the Stockpile Stewardship Program will work or not?

Dr. REIS. First of all, of course, NOVA is working now and is an integral part of our Stockpile Stewardship Program from the laser perspective. We are also using the Omega laser, which builds another part, again, from the laser perspective, in terms of that. Yes; the national ignition facility is a critical part and, while we have every expectation and confidence that it will be built on schedule, as you point out, things do happen and I certainly cannot guarantee that.

But there are other parts of the program that we build up in time. We are doing it now. We will continue to do it. So the problems that show up now we will solve now. As the stockpile ages, we will expect more problems to show up, but we expect to have more capability in time.

What we are talking about now is, if you will, a race against mother nature, and we think we have laid out as best we can what the problems are that we expect to have. We understand a lot about these weapons. We don't expect to understand everything about them. But, again, we have laid out a program that we believe now is sufficient to answer all those questions.

Ultimately, we also have to have built in the safeguards for the stewardship program. That is a part of the program itself.

Senator REID. Senator Cochran, would you yield for just a moment?

Senator COCHRAN. Certainly.

Senator REID. Dr. Reis, in answer to his question, at least as I understand it, he said do you believe the Stockpile Stewardship Program will work, but I did not hear your answer.

Dr. REIS. The answer to that is yes, I do.

Senator REID. Thank you, Senator.

Senator DOMENICI. Senator Cochran, are you finished?

Senator COCHRAN. Yes; I am.

Senator DOMENICI. Thank you very much for attending today. You are on the subcommittee and we thank you for the participation that you are committing to us today. I understand you have a broader based jurisdiction than we do. We are looking at the budget implications and it is obvious that this is not as simple a proposition as some would make it.

Is that not correct from what you know so far?

Senator COCHRAN. Well, I am not a witness, but I would be glad to testify if you wish. [Laughter.]

Senator DOMENICI. No; you don't have to do that. [Laughter.]

On page 7 of the document you asked that we might put into the record—and we have made the whole document attached. Why don't we attach that whole document rather than have it printed. We can just attach it to the record.

[The information follows:]

CAPABILITIES NEEDED TO ENSURE HIGH CONFIDENCE IN WARHEAD SAFETY AND RELIABILITY

Weapons physics	Computer simulation	DARHT	Subcritical experi-ments	NIF	Pulsed power	LANSCE
Improved physical modes	X	X	X	X	X	X
Early implosion	X	X	X	......	......	X
Preboost	X	X	X	X	X	X
Boost	X	......	......	X	......	......
Primary-secondary coupling	X	......	......	X	X	......
Secondary implosion	X	......	......	X	X	......
Weapon performance	X	......	......	......	......	......

Senator DOMENICI. On page 7, I note that you have listed computer simulation, DARHT, subcritical experiments, NIF, pulsed power, and LANSCE.

Dr. REIS. Yes, sir.

Senator DOMENICI. Now in response to Senator Cochran's question regarding NIF, it is the biggest of the projects in terms of a structure and expenditure, is it not—of the program?

Dr. REIS. That's correct.

Senator DOMENICI. Pulsed power, if it proves out, could do some of the things that NIF does. Is that not correct?

Dr. REIS. It is complementary. I think the pulsed power could do some of the things that NIF does. It can do other things that NIF cannot do. NIF can do some things that pulsed power cannot do.

LOS ALAMOS NEUTRON SCIENCE CENTER

Senator DOMENICI. How does LANSCE fit into this?

Dr. REIS. LANSCE is the Los Alamos Neutron Scattering Center, and that is where we use neutrons to really understand the details of using neutron scattering to really get in and look at the details of both the nuclear and nonnuclear parts, the explosion itself.

One of the keys, Senator, is this ability to do surveillance properly. What you would like to be able to do and what we are pushing for, as far as what we call enhanced surveillance, is you would rather not wait until there is a defect and then fix the stockpile. What you really want to do is determine ahead of time: Are there indications that, for example, the high explosive is beginning to change its properties so that we would have to change it out before there is any problem?

To do that, we have to really understand in much greater detail than we do now the material properties. That is where a device, a system like the LANSCE, is particularly effective.

Senator DOMENICI. Dr. Reis, while I have you here, let me just go back to something for 1 minute. It does somewhat involve this but not totally.

Dr. REIS. I think we made a copy of that.

Senator DOMENICI. Fine.

CONFIDENCE IN THE STOCKPILE

In listening to Secretary Schlesinger in the Governmental Affairs hearing, which Senator Cochran chairs, Dr. Schlesinger expressed some grave reservations about the Comprehensive Test Ban Treaty being in our Nation's interest. He argued that continuation of the underground testing program is the only assurance that we can have of the integrity of the stockpile. He also noted that several previous defense chiefs, as well as laboratory directors, several previous ones of both types, have consistently noted the importance of underground testing.

In that same hearing, Dr. Barker, who is a Livermore expert, expressed concern that it will be many years before we will know if the Stockpile Stewardship Program can succeed and in that regard succeed in maintaining the level of confidence we require in our stockpile.

He questioned if national security is well served by entering into a CTBT before we know how the stewardship program will work.

How do you address their concerns that a nation needs an underground testing program to maintain the integrity? If you would like, I will add just a second point to this.

How would you address Dr. Barker that stockpile stewardship cannot be demonstrated to succeed for many years and during that time we will have low capabilities, will have lost our capabilities, under the treaty?

Dr. REIS. Well, I would have to respectfully disagree with both Dr. Barker and at some trepidation with Dr. Schlesinger.

But I would suggest that the reason I feel much more comfortable about it than perhaps they do is I have been working at it for 5 years while previous chiefs have said some time ago that they were concerned about it.

This is a different program. We are now not trying to develop new weapons. We are trying to maintain a stockpile of very well tested and very well understood weapons.

Second, while it may be some years before the full program is in place—I think the program is in place now and it is working now. It has been 5 years since the last weapon was tested. And, as Secretary Peña just said, we have just gone through an extraordinarily detailed second annual certification. While he has not yet signed off, as you said, he expects to be able to sign off on that, as well as Secretary Cohen to sign off fairly soon.

The last reason is one that I think I alluded to in my testimony. I think our laboratories and our plants are now very different places than they were 4 or 5 years ago. Through the Stockpile Stewardship Program we have really been reinvigorated—and I should say with help from you, Senator Domenici, and Senator Reid, and the Congress as well, who have been very supportive in terms of that program.

We have gone through some risks and it has taken quite a bit of courage and resources to do this. So I think if you ask the current laboratory directors, and I'm sure you will, and if you ask the current senior military, and you have some examples here from the civilian leadership as well, you will find that they feel that yes, while there clearly is risk, that risk is well worthwhile in terms of our broad national security interests and that we will be able to maintain those nuclear weapons and the system that supports those nuclear weapons indefinitely. And we have a high probability of being able to do that without testing.

SIGNATORY COUNTRIES TO THE CTBT

Senator DOMENICI. By the way, which countries are signatories to the treaty now?

Mr. MILLER. We can get you the full list. There are 41 countries now.

Dr. REIS. That have ratified at this stage of the game?

Mr. MILLER. No; they are signatories.

I believe 145 have signed. I will get you the full list for your record.

[The information follows:]

As of 31 October 1997, 148 countries have signed the Comprehensive Nuclear Test Ban Treaty (CTBT), and seven have ratified it. The seven are: Czech Republic, Fiji, Japan, Federated States of Micronesia, Mongolia, Qatar, and Uzbekistan. Of the 44 countries named in the Treaty, whose ratification is required for entry into force, all but three—India, Pakistan, and North Korea—have signed the treaty.

Senator DOMENICI. And from those that are commonly known as having nuclear capacity, nuclear weapon capacity, are they all on board?

Mr. MILLER. India and Pakistan are not.

If I could say something about that, I think that if we got to a point where the treaty entered into force even without India and Pakistan—and that would require an extraordinary conference in 3 years time and it would require coming back to the Senate for ratification of a provision that changes the basic treaty, that says the treaty does not enter into force until all the nuclear States and threshold States have ratified—it creates an international norm which even a State like India would break at some significant risk.

And so, if the treaty is in effect, I think it constrains the weapons programs of even those acknowledged States that are not party to the treaty. There is value there.

Senator DOMENICI. That's understandable.

Thank you.

Let me talk about another issue with the two scientists for 1 minute.

DUAL REVALIDATION

In matters such as this, it is very likely that there would be differences of opinion among experts on the health of the stockpile and the weapons that are principally of long-time stockpile nature, and that may require some change in manufacturing or some change in the stockpile weapon. How will differences of opinion be resolved without the ultimate authority of a nuclear test to settle an issue?

Dr. SMITH. I'll take the first stab and will then turn to Victor.

First of all, the process that had been up on the previous chart brings together all the expertise that we have and the debates that have taken place now with 2 years experience in certification are very intense.

I think, in fact, I am positive that every possible expert opinion is heard. It is not a case of taking a vote. It is a case of working through the details. We have found so far that when we work through those details, in fact, we are satisfied that the weapons are safe, secure, and reliable.

But that is not enough. We have also instituted between the two departments what we call dual revalidation, which purposefully and deliberately sets up independent review teams between the two weapons design laboratories—Los Alamos and Livermore. If Los Alamos designed the weapon then Livermore has to create its own independent team to go over the designs, the tests, to recommend new tests, to do new calculations on old data, to do everything they can to form their own independent review.

So this is peer review such as the world has never seen.

I find it hard to believe that between those two processes every opinion that is technically based, that is a true expert opinion, will not be presented. It will be heard, will be discussed, and a consensus I am rather certain will be formed.

Dr. REIS. Let me add two things to that.

First, as you notice, the process has not just a central chain but two chains along the side. So what we have tried to do is insure ourselves—and that reports are sent separately to the Secretary of Defense and to the Secretary of Energy. So we have been very sensitive to insure ourselves the independence of those two groups.

They all work with the same data in terms of their judgments, in terms of their questions. Not only does it work through the process through the Nuclear Weapons Council, but they are also required to give their own separate judgments to the Secretary of Energy and the Secretary of Defense.

So we have been very sensitive to minority opinion.

Let me also add one more thing to this dual revalidation process. Senator Cochran, I think that gets back to the point you were making: How do we know this thing is working?

In addition, one of my main concerns is how do I train the new people. How do we get the new people to understand what went on in the heads and the understanding of the people who actually had the experience in testing and had to do the designing. That is where this dual revalidation comes in.

So not only, if you will, does it insure us literally from going back to the basic information and the basic blueprints and so forth that both these labs are working on with each other, but this is the opportunity for the new people to come along and work with the mentors, work with the people who have actually done the designing over that time. Why did you make this decision? Why did you make that decision? Let's look at the new tools and see if we can predict some of the same results we got from the old data, basically.

This is really the essence of what we are trying to do, bring the new people on so that when the time comes that the old people are gone, you will have had their judgment and expertise. So, again, as you point out, I think correctly, the issue is not now but 10, 15, or 20 years from now. That is when the essence of the idea of the perpetuity of the treaty really comes into force.

Mr. MILLER. Mr. Chairman, if I might just give you an example of how the policy—technical interface works in this area, this dual revalidation is relatively new. Within the past 5 years it came about in part because of the prompting from us in policy.

Previously, Los Alamos looked at its designs and Livermore looked at its designs, but you didn't look at the other guy's designs. Now we broke that wall down because we were concerned about two things: One, getting a new pair of trained, sophisticated scientific eyes on the other person's designs so that potentially new flaws or flaws could be examined; and, second, given the shrinking pool of expertise, we wanted to take advantage, full advantage, of those capabilities that we have, these national resources, these people who have done the testing.

So there was a bit of a push from policy and the technical walls came down, so that people from Los Alamos and Livermore could now get involved in each other's work.

This is an example of the kind of crosscutting work that occurs between all of us.

CTBT SAFEGUARD B—NUCLEAR LABORATORIES

Dr. REIS. Let me pick up if I could on that as well. That is what safeguard B is all about. That is why the specific safeguard B is there, which says you will maintain three nuclear laboratories and you will insure yourself. It specifically talks about the people and the vitality of those laboratories. That is, if you will, the response to the concern that we had from a technical perspective and the concern that policy has. That is put right back into the policy.

As you recall, Senator, there were a number of discussions 2 or 3 years ago where people looking at this asked why do I need all of these laboratories and couldn't I do it with one. The answer is you cannot do it with one because what you really need is that scientific competition to be continually questioning each other with the people from Sandia, Livermore and Los Alamos all working it out. That is just the nature of the scientific method.

They cannot help themselves in competing from a scientific perspective. They are always questioning, always probing each other. It is basically built into their bones. That is just an integral part of the whole stewardship program.

ANNUAL CERTIFICATION

Senator DOMENICI. I note in the previous chart that over on the right hand side you have the three lab directors. I would assume, Dr. Reis and Dr. Smith, that from a technical standpoint, probably their conclusions and their observations would be as important, if not more important, than almost anybody else on that chart.

Is that correct?

Dr. REIS. I would suggest that the institutions that they represent, because the laboratory directors are not necessarily weapons designers, it is their job because they are the ones who have to put their names on it to insure themselves that their institution's integrity is intact. That integrity is just all important to them.

That is why, frankly, I think it is so important to get, if you will, their signature specifically on this and not just as part of a bureaucratic process; that they have to stand up every year and say look, representing my institution, those weapons are safe and reliable—or not. Ultimately, you are dependent upon the integrity and the competence, if you will, of those people.

Senator DOMENICI. What I meant was not the individual person signing it, but if you put up a chart over there with those three people, representing 7,000 to 8,000 of the greatest scientists in the world in each of three laboratories, I assume they go through an exercise whereby their director concludes from the input of that laboratory what he is going to say about certification.

Dr. REIS. Yes.

Senator DOMENICI. That is a very powerful part, I would assume, of this.

Dr. REIS. That is an extraordinarily powerful part.

Senator DOMENICI. Would you agree with that, Dr. Smith?

Dr. SMITH. It is a simple answer that I would like to give.

I would not agree that the laboratory directors or, more appropriately, the institutions they represent are the first among equals. They are equals, though. They are certainly not inferiors.

But we do want the opinions of STRATCOM, we do want the opinions of the Nuclear Weapons Council with all the components that it represents. But the laboratory directors and their institutions are of equal and important input.

Senator DOMENICI. I have just two quick questions.

Do you have some more questions, Senator?

Senator COCHRAN. I just thought of one, if you would let me ask it now.

Senator DOMENICI. Go ahead.

FUTURE FUNDING FOR STOCKPILE STEWARDSHIP VERSUS TESTING

Senator COCHRAN. If you could compare, for example, a nuclear testing program in terms of cost with the stewardship program over the next 20 years, how much money would we save if we did low yield testing instead of the stewardship program?

Dr. REIS. I don't think you could, but you just did low yield testing, you would certainly save money. But if I did not do the stewardship program, I would not be able to maintain the safety, reliability, and performance of the stockpile. I think both Dr. Schlesinger and Dr. Barker so testified. They said fundamental to their discussion is you would still do the stewardship program.

So if once you are doing the stewardship program——

Senator COCHRAN. Would it have to be as expensive as the one we are undertaking?

Dr. REIS. I have looked at that because, indeed, we had to worry about that. I think we have the right, essentially the right program the way it is now. If we have to go back and test or something like that, that is essentially built into the program already.

So I don't think it is a cost issue, Senator. If people looked at the program as, for example, what if we just manufacture and test—I mean, there are other potential solutions to the idea of basically maintaining the stockpile. You know, different countries might do it basically based on their systems.

Based on our system, based on how we are doing it, I think we are doing it the right way. I don't think there are any cost savings to be made. I think we have indicated that we don't think there is any fat, basically any fat in the program. It is hard to project 5, 10, 15, 20 years into the future. But I don't believe one could come up with a program that will do this job for any less money than that.

Senator COCHRAN. Thank you.

Senator DOMENICI. We have 13 minutes left on a vote and I think we need a little time to move you over to the next room to do our closed hearing.

I have a number of other questions that I am going to submit. If you have any, Senator Cochran, you can submit them. Senator Reid also had some.

ONSITE INSPECTION MECHANISM OF CTBT

But I want to just ask you one question about the onsite inspection mechanism provided for in this treaty.

As this treaty unfolds, people are going to go through all parts of it. You all have alluded to a few things that have not been talked about much in public. But there are two ways, obviously, to try to detect the explosion.

One is we were successful in maintaining in this treaty that we could have our own system of detection. Whatever we have by way of satellites or whatever we have, we can keep, and so can other countries. Then there is a system of international ones. Obviously, the question then comes is not an onsite inspection almost always necessary to establish the situs.

I assume, for the most part, you want to actually locate the situs of the explosion if it occurred.

I note in the treaty that 30 of the 51 nation executive councils must agree before an onsite inspection can occur.

Now, I think this is going to be a bone of contention around here and that there are going to be a lot of questions about this aspect. Why such a large number and do you really believe it is going to be easy to get 30 out of that Executive Committee of 51 nations to agree to permit onsite inspections?

Let's start with you, Mr. Miller.

Mr. MILLER. I don't think we know the answer to that, Senator. But on the face of it, given that the vast majority of the members are not nuclear weapons states, I don't see that there is a built in reason why it would be difficult to get 30. They are not protecting anything if they are not testing, and if one of the states is testing, then it is a minority of one.

There will undoubtedly be controversy. This is a mechanism that is going to have to be worked out, just like any other treaty mechanism is going to have to be worked out. But on the face of it, I do not believe that that is going to be a problem. I could be proven wrong, but I don't believe so.

Senator DOMENICI. Do you have a comment on that, Dr. Smith?

Dr. SMITH. If the evidence is close to incontrovertible and the abilities we will have will strongly suggest that an explosion of some magnitude takes place, then it would be very hard, I would think, to resist the chance of a nation that feels it has been unjustly treated to insist on an inspection. And, as Mr. Miller has pointed out, there will be plenty of nations in the 50 that would welcome the chance.

But as to the difficulty, I rather imagine it will be hard. But you, far more than Mr. Miller and I, are well aware of how ones tries to get 31 votes out of 50.

Senator DOMENICI. Yes; I try to get 51 out of 100.

Senator COCHRAN. We have to get 60.

Senator DOMENICI. Yes; sometimes 60. It can be very difficult.

I do have an observation. I was told, and by people that I am sure do know, that the reason for 30 is because that was part of the bargaining to maintain in the treaty the national technical means aspect of this treaty. And the swap-out was OK, if you insist on keeping your own national means, then we are going to go more than a simple majority or more than a big minority allowing the onsite inspections.

Frankly, I don't know why we needed the tradeoff. If we need to go to a country, at least we know from our standpoint we are not going out there to look for something to learn, to take away from them. We are trying to find out whether or not this happened.

So I am not so sure about the statement that we have equipment and technology to discern whether or not an explosion has occurred. I would remind all of you of the situation in Russia in Novaya Zemlya. We are still arguing about whether there was an explosion there or not. We are not absolutely certain there wasn't.

Dr. SMITH. Mr. Chairman, we are not arguing about where that event took place.

Senator DOMENICI. That's right. But all they would have to say to this council of 51 is we don't think it happened and here is our evidence. Why do we want to let this team come in and inspect?

That is the reason I raised the point. It would take a long time to agree on that.

CONCLUSION OF HEARING

Our open meeting stands in recess. We will resume in close session across the hall in about 10 minutes.

Thank you.

[Whereupon, at 4:40 p.m., Wednesday, October 29, the hearing was concluded, and the subcommittee was recessed, to reconvene subject to the call of the Chair.]

○

